Veracity At Its Best

Michele Doucette

Veracity At Its Best

ISBN 978-1-935786-01-6

Printed in the United States of America by

St. Clair Publications

PO Box 726

McMinnville, TN   37111-0726

http://stan.stclair.net

Acknowledgments

As a writer, it is of the utmost importance to write about what you know, what you feel, what you believe, for in doing so, the intended audience will be able to feel, and resonate with, the deep passion put forth in the words on the page.

Not always knowing from where the words have come, it is my belief that the *universal, infinite, loving mind* of this energetic cosmos has continued to guide me, and for that I am eternally grateful.

Awake. Be the witness of your thoughts. You are what observes, not what you observe.

Buddha

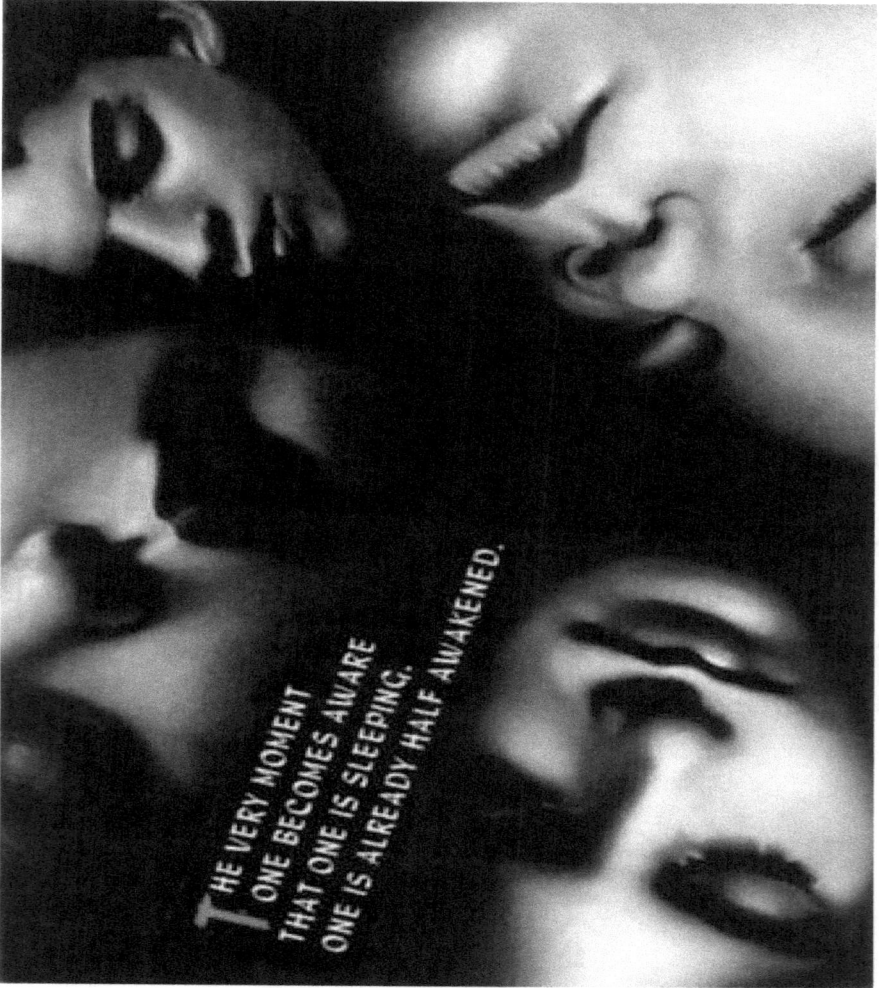

THE VERY MOMENT ONE BECOMES AWARE THAT ONE IS SLEEPING, ONE IS ALREADY HALF AWAKENED.

Sleepers Awaken © Claire Lewis Evans
Reprinted with permission.

Table of Contents

Author's Note

Veracity comes from the Latin word *veritas*, meaning verifiable truth. Upon honest reflection, the only constant in life is change; all is constantly unfolding and expanding. While there was a time when I feared change, I now look forward to evolving.

The next constant is that of truth. In keeping, this work is *a study of my own truth.*

Truth is naught but a relative term, meaning that truth is different for each individual. Every person wrestles with this concept, all in an attempt to ascertain that which they uphold.

One of the most challenging tasks we face is to learn to become nonjudgmental. It is important to remember that all of us are *continually evolving and changing* as per our own individual experience(s).

While many continue to accept limiting thoughts, of which there are a significant number (including fear, guilt, despair, unworthiness, failure, worry, unhappiness, pity, misery, hatred, dissension, denial of self), into their lives, it must be remembered that this is neither good nor bad. Coming from a place of nonjudgment, it simply is.

While all things are derived from thought, which I equate with God, it is equally important to realize that God is not simply one formulated thought, but the reality of *all* thoughts. Individual truths, then, as held by you, as held by me, are *all* true, for each expresses the truth(s) of one's experience at any given moment in time.

While there is *truth in all things*, so, too, is there *refinement in all things*. In fact, each moment serves to refine truth, which is why I believe that God is *not* a state of perfection, but rather a state of Becoming.

Only *you* can be the giver of your own truth. It is a feeling, a knowingness. To *know* your truth is also to *feel* your truth. Seek what feels right within your soul. Believe in yourself, for your truth also contributes to that of the collective.

Quite simply, *veracity at its best* is all about co-creation, co-truth, co-truthfulness.

It is important to be willing to Become unlimited in your truth, remembering, always, that truth is ongoing, evolving, being created every moment by every thought you have.

Veracity At Its Best

When you have come to understand that *everything* is true and yet *nothing* is true, for therein lies the paradox, you shall be able to see that just as you perceive truth to be whatever you determine it to be, so may all.

In continuation, in the moment that you no longer give credence to a truth, it is no longer real, for you have since moved toward a new truth.

Henceforth, when you come to understand that truth *is* and *can be* all things, then you are free, no longer enslaved to laws, rules, dogma or intellectual understanding.

To learn to Become multi-faceted in your truth means that you are not *one* truth, but *all* truths.

Change allows all to Be (as they are) and to Become (who they truly are).

Do not try to restrict others by judging them, controlling them or blaming them, for this limits your understanding of them. By direct association, this behavior also serves to limit their understanding of themselves.

Just as you have experienced yours, so, too, must you allow others the time and opportunity to experience their own freedom, their own resolution, moving forward as best they know how.

Veracity At Its Best

When you respond to people with love and compassion, you readily move from conflict to harmony. Such is the very freedom sought by all. When you remember, embrace and share your divinity, you free others to walk their truth. You become accepting of their truth, for such is whom they are.

As for myself, I was so sure that the way to gnosis, nirvana and enlightenment was through a multitude of books and CD programs, metaphysical tools and spiritual teachers.

It feels so much more liberating to know that, whilst all of these may come into one's life, they merely serve to help each person develop, strengthen and acknowledge their own inner teacher.

Clearly, what all are seeking exists *within*.

In order to best ascertain your inner truth, you have to look with both the outer physical eye, taking all in as an astute and objective observer, as well as with the inner eye (better known as the third eye).

Truth at its best is, indeed, veracity at its best; hence the aptness of the title.

There are people in my life that I would like to acknowledge herein, for they, in their own way, have contributed to my growth along the spiritual path.

To my husband, Albert Stewart, who steadily encourages me to write. After twenty-five years, he continues to remain my confidant, my anchor, my companion.

To my children, Alyssa and Niall. May they, too, be blessed in their young lives with love, laughter and genuine friendship.

To my mother, Anne, and my sisters, Cathy, Lynette, Denise and Andrea, all of whom fully support my writing efforts, even though they may not comprehend the path I have chosen.

To those who need to be recognized for their deeply inspirational and spiritual contributions to my life ……

Michelle Anderson, a star sister, who continues to support my every effort, stating that I am both messenger and master at connecting people with the information they seek and need.

Karen Quinton Bennett, a local spiritual companion who also resonates deeply with the Starseed stone of choice: Moldavite.

Nannette Blondet, an inquisitive soul sister, dedicated to finding and sharing the truth.

Linda Earle, a local soul sister who demonstrates the strength of the female Celtic warrior, Boudicca, a name meaning *victorious*.

Robert Ray, a dear friend and companion who is dedicated to the idea of energy independence and saving Mother Earth.

Elio Serra, an old soul companion who takes the time to be completely honest and loving.

David Shirk, a soul brother, and fellow teacher, who is successfully disengaging from the Matrix.

To Jon Law for permission to use his *Nefertiti* photograph as the cover image. Long have I been intrigued with this historical personage. You can find other images on Flickr at http://www.flickr.com/photos/12113806@N04/2974685601/in/set-72157602856465482/

To Claire Lewis Evans for permission to avail of her photograph entitled *Sleepers Awaken* as such just seemed to be so appropriate. Please take the time to visit her website at http://www.clairelewisevans.com as well as her Flickr site http://www.flickr.com/photos/clairelewisevans/3553122440

As people come together, one comes to the realization that it really *is* an incredibly small world, orchestrated with much synchronicity, if one pays attention to the signs.

If I may now leave you with some words to ponder ……

To offer no resistance to life is to be in a state of grace, ease, and lightness. This state is then no longer dependent upon things being a certain way, good or bad. It seems almost paradoxical, yet when your inner dependency on form is gone, the general conditions of your life, the outer forms, tend to improve greatly. Things, people, or conditions that you thought you needed for your happiness now come to you with no struggle or effort on your part, and you are free to enjoy and appreciate them – while they last. All those things, of course, will still pass away, cycles will come and go, but with dependency gone there is no fear of loss anymore. Life flows with ease.

Eckhart Tolle

In addition, what one resists always persists and does not go away; hence, the despondency as well as the dependency.

Clearly, this is something else upon which to reflect.

Reviews

Veracity At Its Best by Michele Doucette constructs the context for the spiritual message the author imparts in *A Travel in Time to Grand Pré*. Facet by facet, the author reveals her *philosophy of self-empowerment* through a variety of perspectives. Among Michele's offerings, there will be those that speak directly to the reader's experience, as the chapter entitled The Power of Positive Thinking appealed to mine.

In this time of outrageous consequence, Michele *motivates the reader* to separate from destructive external forces, look inward and create positive ways forward.

Marie Rundquist, author of *Revisiting Anne Marie: How an Amerindian Woman of Seventeenth Century Nova Scotia and a DNA Match Redefine American Heritage*

When I read Michele Doucette's latest work, *Veracity At Its Best*, I realized that one is in danger of facing the one thing that most would rather never face: *the truth about who and what we are.* Who dares ask such questions of the universe?

Veracity literally means *the power of perceiving truth.* Truth can only be experienced from within, given that the universe is already suffused with truth. Only those who dare not ask (the only question that can possibly be asked) do not know the power of veracity.

Veracity might best be summed up as just asking one simple question: Who am I? My answer is simply this. I AM.

In continuation, I AM is ONE. I AM is ALL. ALL is ONE. ONE is I AM. Therefore, as stated before: I AM.

Whether you need to breathe, increase your energetic vibration, or rid yourself of toxic thought cycles, the well written pages of *Veracity At Its Best* can serve as a guide in a region that may be unfamiliar.

Do you, the reader, actually want to know the truth or do you just want to go ahead with life as before?

Go ahead. Be not afraid to ask the question, for the answer will remove both the question and the answer, leaving only the simple, unvarnished truth.

To perceive the truth is to become the truth. To become the truth is, indeed, to live veracity at its best as outlined herein by Michele Doucette.

If you want to know the truth, just ask the question so that you, too, can discover.

David Shirk, USA

Michele is extraordinary ... there are jewels to be found in every chapter. Put aside all other self-help, new age or spiritual books because this one captures it all.

The meaning of life is explained in simple, yet powerful terms.

Even better, the reader is encouraged to wake up from the deep slumber (or spell) humanity has been under for ages. The pertinent question, then, becomes ... is this what you want?

Jean-Guy Poirier, Canada

In many respects, I am reminded of *ancient Buddhist wisdom* as I read through this book. True wisdom endures the ages, and, indeed, the ideas that Michele speaks of are *enduring* and *timeless*.

To know that the energies we project are returned to us, to know that we are spiritual beings having a physical experience, to know that as the universe aligns so must we; all leads us into preparedness for the alignment of 2012 that will soon be upon us.

Perhaps most of the world will not take notice. Nothing will change, at least not outwardly. But for those who can prepare themselves and begin aligning their energies now, during 2012 they will have heightened experiences that will transcend mind and matter. The alignments assure us that, if we are in tune, the possibilities are endless and miraculous.

Michele is a seductive writer whose *words flow like prose* on each page. A compassionate and persuasive guide, she gently leads us, as a parent would guide a child, benevolently, through life's training.

Knowing that I could trust this author to lead me tenderly and wisely, she did not disappoint me.

I highly recommend this book as a much easier, handy little guide for the spiritual and metaphysical course that is now unfolding before our very eyes.

Suzanne Olsson, author of *Jesus In Kashmir, The Lost Tomb*

As a child growing up, our view of the world is created by our parents and other caretakers. For most of us, we conclude that we live only one life, and that, depending on the kind of life we live, at death, will either go to heaven or hell. This author has presented a *compelling case* to suggest that this may not be true at all.

Raising fundamental issues (*who are we* and *why are we here*), she also speaks of the elements of our physical experience. She further addresses many concepts and levels of consciousness, all of which would suggest that not only are we far more than we ever imagined, but that we also experience many lifetimes of existence.

This book will *challenge your ability to have an open mind*; a mind that would allow you to disregard all you have learned so that you may create a new view of life, and who you may become.

Taking a very complicated subject, this author presents it in easy to read steps. One could think of it as an *Instruction Manual on Life*.

If you want to know what is really going on around you, I strongly suggest that you read this *very informative* book. In doing so, you will expand your consciousness to a new and exciting level.

Richard E. Guertin, USA

Spiritual author Michele Doucette, in her gripping new book, *Veracity At Its Best*, has presented a unique viewpoint on awakening the divine spark within each of us.

Contrary to the common new age teaching of the higher consciousness or God consciousness, Michele teaches how we can understand the true inner man/woman, determine who we really are, and overcome our perceived limitations.

Michele herein addresses several important questions in dealing with becoming all that we can, and should, become in order to experience life at its fullest.

Is it possible to shut out negativity and reprogram our minds?

How do we become more positive in our thinking, and what will we experience by doing so?

What is mindfulness and how do we achieve it?

How do we eliminate an attitude of judgmental thinking, and begin to really love ourselves, and others, unconditionally, regardless of our past actions, thoughts or belief systems?

How do we relate to ego, and how does this relate to our understanding of life?

Are we separate or connected?

How can we become more aware of the world around us, achieving freedom from the egoic mind?

How can we develop a burning desire and have the things we want?

In what way were we created in the image of God?

How are we creators?

What will 2012 bring?

Michele maintains that positive metamorphosis is very achievable, introducing her readers to solid and workable principles which, when practiced daily, will enable their fulfillment.

A striking journey into the mastery of compassion and the enrichment of real Self.

Discover how to shift your thinking and your focus, turn negative energy into positive energy, expand your mind, design your own reality and positively impact your future. *Veracity At Its Best* is a *very deep, pensive study* into Michele's beliefs regarding truth, spiritual enlightenment and our relationship with the Universe.

Stanley J. St. Clair, author of *Prayers of Prophets, Knights and Kings* and *Mysterious People of the Bible in the Light of History*

Michèle Doucette, with whom I am honored to be a sister on the path to light, has written a *comprehensive book* about the spiritual path. It is *clearly written* and *easy to read.*

Michèle is so right when she says that teachers, CDs and books are merely transformative tools. At some point, we all have to move forward, trusting our inner Self. This is perhaps the most important point that Michèle makes.

The next most important point pertains to standing firm against fear. She writes: *I refuse to exist within the framework of fear. It shall be in the standing firm of this resolve, that I can better assist those around me who can see no other way.*

Michèle has drawn on a vast range of teachings and resources in order to present *a clear synthesis of the truth,* as she sees it, along with what we can do to reach our truth.

This book is *a message of self-liberation.*

This book is *a message of love.*

Everyone possesses an individual part of the puzzle, and we are now able to see, more and more clearly, the overall picture that these individual pieces are making.

I thoroughly recommend this book. There are enough references to keep you interested and searching on your own path for a long time, so you certainly will not be bored.

Above all, it is *simply written, clear and precise.* This is intended as a compliment to Michèle.

Jacqueline Lion, Certified Astrologist, Pendé, France

While I remember being told at different times in my life that there is *only one truth*, I had no idea what the depth of that statement really meant. I would often use those words, only one truth, to apply to the small things in life quite easily; but the larger meaning of that statement eluded me for the longest time.

The shift in consciousness that this age seems to be requiring of us has begun; and will continue to increase in its pressing demands.

It is time for reeducation and a new understanding to emerge. If we choose to become enlightened and aware, we are given new and effective tools to use; and are expected to master these tools as they appear.

Once completed, we will be entrusted with the next, and even greater, tool. If we resist; our lessons become more challenging, thereby increasing our own needs. This appears to become even more magnified, the more we resist.

Yes, there *is* only one truth; and that is the path we are to follow; but we must first realize that the *real truth*, unfolding before us, *is not dependent upon any prior concepts that we may have been taught as being true.*

What is at the core of this new enlightenment is that we must really learn that *ego weakens us*. What we must learn to accomplish is the opening of our eyes and our hearts in complete trust, thereby allowing truth to surface in the things that challenge us.

Scientists realize that things are changing; and they inherently tend to predict the worst. They are foraging the earth, collecting crop seeds to store in their global deep freeze storage facilities (to preserve the capacity of this moment) in order to feed the multitudes of people in the future.

While their goals are not evil or bad, their efforts are a waste of energies. It may be that they are clueless as to the real reason for this shift and what is being shown to us.

What is required is a new heart; a new concern; a new behavior. As this shift becomes more accepted; the lessons shall become more gentle. The world will begin to reshape and Mother Earth will begin to cooperate.

Many of us could use a manual or a lesson plan.

Veracity at Its Best is part of my lesson plan, pointing me in a better direction. This resource is helping me become more aware of my role in this paradigm shift. I have had to learn that what is good for me is also good for all life forms. Like you, I, too, have my own job to do.

Life continues to be an exciting lesson that challenges my education; but it is proving to be more true than anything I have ever learned before. I wish you a gentle lesson.

Robert Ray, Zero Point Continuum of Life co-founder

Long have I had a keen fascination with Pharaoh Akhenaton, deemed the heretic king, and Queen Nefertiti (an Egyptian name meaning *the beautiful one who has come*), co-regent and Great Wife.

Made famous by the bust currently housed in the Altes Museum in Berlin, part of the Ägyptisches Museum Berlin collection, if such is a true likeness, clearly she must have been beautiful enough to have deserved such a name. To date, this bust is among the most recognized works of art to survive, intact, from the ancient world.

Pharaoh Akhenaton was a revolutionary, most notably made famous for his religious reforms, whereby the polytheism of Egypt was supplanted by monotheism centered around the Aten, the life giving force of light (symbolized as rays of light extending from the disk of the sun).

With relief illustrations depicting the Aten as being a three-dimensional spherical shape, it was the late scholar Hugh Nibley that suggested globe, orb or sphere was a more correct translation for the Aten as opposed to a flat disk.

It needs to be mentioned here that Akhenaton means *illuminated manifestation of Aten*.

This new religion, foisted upon the Egyptian populace, involved the pharaoh and his family forming the link between god and the ordinary people, with Akhenaton claiming to be the sole intimate of the Aten theology.

Akhenaton assumed the role of High Priest of the Aten, ably assisted by Nefertiti and their young daughters. Accorded a degree of prominence that no other major civilization in the ancient world was willing to concede to a woman, it appears that he may well have established the first triad involving himself, the Aten and Nefertiti.

Why did Akhenaton feel a need for such a religious revolution?

Knowing that the Amun priesthood were the largest landowners in the country might well have had something to do with it. It is highly possible that he feared there might be a rise of a parallel government, one that might threaten his own monarchy. It is as equally possible that this particular monarchy couple were motivated by their shared belief in a single god, a single entity, wanting to make such the official religion of Egypt. While we may never know, truly a religious revolution it was.

Standing on the 21st century precipice of a spiritual revolution, we are also being called upon to challenge the status quo, to challenge previously held beliefs, to seek the truth(s) that live within, while making use of personal discernment along the way.

In the words of John Lennon, a revolutionary ahead of his time, while *we all want to change the world*, I am hoping that the reading of this tome may begin to provide you, the reader, with some semblance as to the real solutions needed to begin the freeing of your mind.

As my friend, Ivan Fraser of The Truth Campaign shares … *The bigger the lie, the more people will believe it. If you know the truth, then you cannot be taken in by the lie. However, if you believe lies, then all you will find is evidence to reinforce the illusion. The only solution is a truly open mind, a willingness to shed one's dogmas no matter how dearly cherished, and absolute honesty.*

The only question that bodes asking is … are you ready?

The Breath: The First Miracle

Take a few moments to contemplate the wonder of breathing. In and out. In and out. In and out. It is imperative that we take the time to *truly appreciate* the first miracle of life, all courtesy of the power of the breath.

In truth, we must become more *mindful* of this exquisite gift, a gift beyond measure, a gift that many have a tendency to take completely for granted.

Without attempting to achieve transcended awareness, one can experience a *change in consciousness* when they take five to ten minutes, per day, to concentrate solely on the process of breathing.

Find a comfortable place where you shant be disturbed. Feel free to listen to a musical selection that relaxes you without taking your focus away from the breathing exercise.

Sitting with a straight back, take a deep breath, slowly and naturally, expanding the diaphragm as you fill your lungs to capacity. Hold the breath for a count of ten before releasing. Once again, take a deep breath, hold for a count of ten and then release.

Upon completion, you will find yourself in a different state of mind. What a wonderful way to begin and/or end each day.

In taking this to another level, Adrian Cooper, author of a book called *Our Ultimate Reality: Life, the Universe, and the Destiny of Mankind*, manages a website whereby one can subscribe to a weekly newsletter.

In was in the May 16, 2010 installment located at http://www.ourultimatereality.com/newsletters/160510.pdf whereby he took the time to address the issue of *right breathing*, stating that most people are not aware that the process of breathing has significance far beyond merely supplying the physical body with ample oxygen.

There are three fundamental ways in which we breathe: [1] from the neck and shoulders (the most shallow form of breathing), [2] from the chest (the way most healthy people breathe), and [3] from the solar plexus (the most profound and *spiritual* way of breathing).

In keeping with the Yogi's of India, the Monks of Tibet, and the Martial Arts Masters of Japan, Cooper shares that their powers come from one fundamental purpose: to unite with and express Source; a process that is very much associated with *right breathing*.

While Olympic athletes know the importance of controlled breathing, few practice right breathing. While those who meditate know the importance of deep relaxation, few actually practice right breathing. In summation, right breathing, according to Cooper, is the source of all physical, mental and spiritual power.

Situated just below the navel (belly button) is the solar plexus. Cooper then goes on to share that … "just as the navel is our point of connection with the Source of Life in the Womb through which we are nourished and sustained by the Mother, the corresponding Solar Plexus Chakra is our point of Connection with the Womb of the Universe from and through which we are expressed – the Source of All That Is" … meaning that right breathing serves to facilitate the flow of Universal life energy when the solar plexus chakra has been appropriately developed.

It is imperative, then, that we learn to make the solar plexus the focus center of our breathing.

Cooper shares the directions to right breathing.

1. Inhale for as long and as deeply as you can in through your nose, with your mouth closed. Ensure that this inhalation is long, smooth and progressive. Continue this inhalation until you feel your lungs are as full as possible without discomfort.

2. Now *press* that Breath down to your abdomen, the location of your navel, really feeling your abdominal region expanding with the pressure as much as you can without feeling excessive discomfort. You should feel this breath now firmly centered in the region of your navel, knowing this to be true.

3. With your centre of focus remaining on the breathe in your abdominal area, part your lips slightly and exhale very slowly through your mouth, always feeling and knowing that you are exhaling from the abdominal area where your mind is focused. This slow release of breath should last at least 10 seconds, 15 seconds is better.

While a person may feel discomfort at first, Cooper further advises one to persevere in the knowledge that they will soon become used to this right breathing until it becomes natural.

He also shares that you may feel various sensations due to the much greater Universal life energy flow. It is important that you treat these as positive confirmations of success.

Everything is comprised of energy. Everything is vibration. All vibration is the result of energy in motion. Energy is held together to create matter. Matter is energy condensed to a slow vibration.

There is one underlying field of energy, the Zero Point Field, that pervades everything, thereby giving purpose and unity to our world.

Everything in the universe has a unique vibrational energy. Every object, every being, every thought, every action, every psychological mood; in short, *energy equals vibration.*

Energy and vibration are what life is all about. We can use our energy to help others. We can feel the energy when we meditate. We are also able to feel the energy (life force) inside our bodies on a daily basis, just through the wonder of breathing.

In addition, harmonic resonance between fields of consciousness (meaning the minds of people) can be realized when their rates of vibration are similar.

As spiritual beings inhabiting a physical body, each has their own vibratory signature.

The quality of one's vibratory signature depends on both their thoughts and their inner mental (feeling) world.

If one feels inadequate, insecure and lacking in self esteem, this results in an inward withdrawal. These individuals tend to become engulfed in a negative inner dialogue, one that is embodied by self-pity.

It is this very negative vibration that emanates outward. In accordance with the Law of Attraction, this negative energy will only attract more of the same.

No matter how much this person seeks happiness and success in their life, they continue to feel more and more like a dismal failure, at anything and everything.

They may not understand that it is one's inner world that must ultimately be changed before such can be duly reflected in the outer world of which they are a part.

Focus and concentration are major keys with respect to the changing of one's inner world.

It is your energy vibration that attracts corresponding circumstances (be they people, places, things or events) into your life.

By the same token, it is your energy vibration that can ultimately change your reality.

We are constantly projecting our thought patterns. If one is *conscious* of these thought patterns, then they are creating by *deliberate intent.* If one is *unconscious* of these thought patterns, then they are *creating by default.*

Quite simply, the higher, lighter and purer one's energy vibration frequency, the more that individual is able to tap into the spiritual energy of who they really are.

Many are familiar with the words… *we are not human beings having a spiritual experience; we are spiritual beings having a human experience.* These words belong to Teilhard de Chardin (1881–1955), a philosopher, and Jesuit priest, who was also trained as both a paleontologist as well as a geologist.

It was also de Chardin who said *you are not a human being in search of a spiritual experience; you are a spiritual being immersed in a human experience.*

We are spiritual beings. I am the proprietor of my soul, just as you are the proprietor of your own, and yet there exists a shared destiny within all of us: to sincerely identify with the fact that the *peaceable kingdom* exists within.

How, then, does one advance towards this peaceable kingdom?

One begins by opening up and saying yes to life.

A word of significant power, take the time, now, to say the word yes in your mind. Say it several times, getting louder with each utterance. Are you able to feel the energy shift? Are you able to feel the energy expanse?

When I say yes to life, I feel more joyful, more exuberant, more alive.

Now take the time to compare the difference in saying yes in your mind with saying yes, with strength and conviction, out loud to the Universe.

If it is your intent to open up on a wonderfully energetic level, *this* is the way that you can begin to do so.

The Universe continues to offer a multitude of opportunities and experiences in which to say yes.

Not only that, but every time you both welcome and are open to what shows up in your life, your energy field shifts to a yes vibration.

Saying yes to life positions you in a completely different venue.

You will find that you are now *open to experiencing the totality of all that life has to offer*.

The more one is able to remain open to a given experience, relaxing and embracing the situation at hand, doing their best to learn from the event itself, the easier it becomes to transcend, thereby allowing one to move beyond the experience in question.

Whatever you resist *will* persist, as the saying goes. It was Carl Jung who uttered these wise words. He was a man who clearly understood that what you think about recreates itself within your own life experience(s).

Negative energies, then, will only begin to dissipate in the welcoming, accepting and embracing of that which you want to change.

Allow this wisdom to guide you toward embracing the totality of all life.

Most are familiar with the saying that *the outer world is your mirror*, always reflecting yourself back to you. This simply means that your outer world is a direct reflection of your inner world.

If you embrace and feel love, peace, unison and truth, vibrating such throughout the entirety of your being, you will experience people (places, things or events) who feel and reflect the same.

If, on the other hand, all you experience in your outer world is disharmony, aggression, hate, separation and falsehood, you will experience people (places, things or events) who feel and reflect the same.

Much inner healing is needed in order to correct the imbalances that exist. The freeing of the ego can only take place when such a healing has occurred.

As you are meandering this new and unexplored territory, it is important that you make a conscious effort to be *gentle with yourself* while asking the following questions.

What do I love about myself?

What is it that I wish to change?

It is imperative that you take the time to practice the Golden Rule, *treating yourself as you would have others treat you.*

Accepting the premise that you, and you alone, are 100% responsible for the changes that you wish to impart upon your being, is also critical.

I am here to tell you that it is possible to transcend situations in your outer world, all through the shifting of your inner terrain. However, this is *not* something that happens overnight. It is a process that requires work, effort and diligence on your part, of that you can be sure.

While it is not known to whom the following quote can be attributed, it is well worth citing herein.

The good you find in others, is within you as well. The faults you find in others, are your faults as well. After all, to recognize something in your outer world, you must have a reference point in your inner world. The world around you is a reflection, a mirror showing you the person you are. To change your world, simply change yourself. See the best in others, and you will be at your best. Give to others, and you give to yourself. Love others, and you will be loved. Seek to understand, and you will be understood. Listen, and your voice will be heard. Teach, and you will learn.

Clearly, this is the wisdom that needs to understood, that needs to be internalized, that needs to be lived.

We live in a world of infinite possibilities. That having been said, this array continues to take form based on one's thoughts, feelings and emotions.

Unfortunately, our 3D minds struggle with the truth that we are limitless beings. They seem unable to fathom that we are connected to a Source of infinite power and consciousness.

Quite literally, this means that we have the ability to manifest that which we desire.

As one learns to let go of the limiting mind, one begins to experience what it means, as an awesome spiritual being, to have access to infinite possibilities.

While this seems to be a case of far easier said than done, it *does* take time and it *does* get easier. Taking the time to approach it one day at a time is how you will begin to experience the precise unfolding that is needed.

In order to fully embrace *who* we really are, it becomes imperative that each individual must throw off the yoke of repression, the yoke of separation, the yoke of illusion.

Limits exist only in the mind, a mind that has been programmed to believe in repression, separation and illusion.

In the deepest of realities, we are infinite beings that never die. As a result, we have access to infinite experiences and manifestations, all of which can be found through the transcending of the mind.

Given that all souls are sparks of the divine, of the God/dess, all of humanity is an expanded form of God/dess.

Possessing both divine intelligence and freedom of will, we, too, are forever expanding. This means, quite simply, that God/dess is forever expanding through us.

Ramtha says that it is only in becoming God/man and God/woman (by becoming a part of humanity) that we are God/dess realized in the form of matter. Mind you, most have a hard time accepting that we, too, are gods. Perhaps this is because we simply cannot fathom that we are divine.

When one embraces humanity in the physical form, *one is wholly experiencing God/dess*. It is the physical body, therefore, that is the experience.

It must also be stated, however, that the physical body, is not the personality. While the personality is also part of the physical experience, it is not who we are.

We are infinite consciousness.

Infinite consciousness has no body. Infinite consciousness has no form. Infinite consciousness simply is.

That having been said, I am the creator of my own reality.

There are but two options open to each and everyone. One is based on fear, guilt and control. The other is based on love, empathy, compassion and understanding.

What I am here to experience may not be what you are here to experience, and, yet, all experiences are valid.

I have been able to come to the conclusion that everything I need already exists within.

I have no need of any Guru telling me what needs to be done. I have no need of any psychic telling where to go to avoid the much predicted, doom and gloom, Apocalypse.

I refuse to exist within the framework of fear. It shall be in the standing firm of this resolve, that I can better assist those around me who can see no other way.

Opportunities do not happen by chance. Everything that happens in the Universe starts with intention.

Even though an opportunity may present itself, many still are doing their best to deal with the limiting thoughts and beliefs that may stop them from forging ahead.

This is why it becomes so imperative to *learn to become aware* of the thoughts and beliefs that may be limiting your experience(s).

All must work toward resolving and changing.

While there are many who use the term coincidence, I prefer to use synchronicity. Synchronicities, then, are special messages that the Universe sends out to help you manifest your intention(s).

The more you acknowledge these *individualized and personalized messages*, the clearer their meaning shall become.

These signs from the heavens need to be accepted with both gratitude and trust. We are not here to be led astray. When you believe that the Universe shall provide for your every need, it becomes so.

If the Zero Point Field (ZPF) is free and boundless, then, so, too, are we. Everything is interconnected within this life force that flows through the Universe.

Truly, what we have elected to experience here on planet Earth is both holy and divine.

It is in the transcending of the mind, better known as the ego, that we are able to begin to embrace the vastness of all life.

One must, first of all, take the time to *witness the mind*.

This involves becoming aware of your thoughts, your beliefs, your actions. You must then come to understand, at a deeply conscious level, that *you are not your mind*. In and of itself, this is a monumental step.

How, then, does one turn off the egoic mind (so called when controlled by the ego) and tune into the divinity of who you are?

Perhaps the meaning of *Learn deeply of the mind and its mystery for therein lies the true secret of immortality* [Bushby, Tony. (2003) The Secret in the Bible, page 6. Queensland, AU: Joshua Books] actually refers to one's consciousness as opposed to one's mind, for there exists a significant difference between the two.

It is in transcending the mind that one experiences consciousness.

In reality, all authentic teachings are talking to you, as consciousness, for that is the authentic self; they are not talking to you, as mind, as the egoic self.

The mind has a tendency to cloud one's judgment, one's thinking, one's experiencing. Is this what might actually be referred to as *being asleep*?

The most important distinction that can be made is the one that exists between consciousness and mind. Essentially, then, you are also making the distinction between yourself (consciousness) and everything else (the mind).

There are two questions that need to be answered.

Firstly, what is consciousness?

Secondly, what is mind?

Let us first start off with the definition for consciousness.

To *experience and/or have consciousness* means that one must be *aware of something*.

Things get very murky, even for me, when faced with terms such as *higher* consciousness, *objective* consciousness, *Buddhic* consciousness, *cosmic* consciousness, *God* consciousness and *Christ* consciousness, to cite a few.

Truth be told, the very subject of consciousness is something that has been debated for thousands of years. Likewise, it shall continue to be debated for thousands to come.

The achieving of pure consciousness equates to the reaching of an inner state, thereby achieving something that you can keep with you as you go about your day to day living in the now.

However, having accomplished one successful attempt in the experiencing of this state, this stillness, this total connectedness, this oneness, does not equate to complete and total enlightenment.

It becomes the daily maintaining of the awareness, the daily living of the awareness, the alignment with oneness, that you learn to become enlightened.

Therein lies the intention to transcend.

Therein lies the commitment to the authentic self.

Therein lies the *real* you, living in physical manifestation.

While the word mind *entertains thought and will*, there are different levels of mind. Thought, therefore, appears to be a function of the mind.

Rational mind is what all seem to subscribe to, although there are those who would say that some are incapable of rational thought processes.

The conscious mind pertains to one's subjective experiences.

The unconscious mind, also called the subconscious, refers to that part of the mind that one can access through meditation. There are many who believe that affirmations can be used to harness the power of the subconscious mind in order to make desired changes to the conscious mind.

Universal mind refers to the collective cosmic intelligence that pervades everything. As such, the universal mind can also be accessed via meditation.

Most people are *enslaved by their thoughts*, thereby *creating by default* (creation by way of an unconscious means).

It simply does not occur to them that they can free themselves from the chatter of the mind.

Everyday life, for the multitude, seems to be fraught with worry, tension, anxiety and fear. Thoughts arise in one's mind that serve to reflect these outer feelings.

There can be no peace of mind, no stillness, when one is engulfed by such negativity, and, yet, inner peace is within reach of each and every individual. Therein lies the seeming juxtaposition, if you will.

When the mind is silent, happiness reigns inside and out. It is to one's advantage to be able to still the incessant and compulsive chatter of the mind.

The majority are so deeply ingrained within the confines of the human race that they often defer their thinking to someone other than themselves. How, then, can they break free so as to regain control of their own mind?

In order to make this necessary change, one first has to become aware of the problem. One then must work, consciously, toward reconfiguring how one thinks, how one responds, how one acts.

Not an easy process, it does take time, and all who elect to travel this path (most often, a solitary one) must be commended for their choice(s).

Making the decision to advance on the spiritual path, is not always an easy one. Therefore, one must remain firm in their resolve to do so.

To stop acting, instinctively, on the prompt of each and every thought … this is the gateway to enlightenment.

To cleanse the mind completely, to make it silent … this is the gateway to enlightenment.

To become a completely conscious being … this is the gateway to enlightenment.

As one demonstrates congruence among consciousness, thoughts, feelings, emotions, speech and actions, one becomes more satisfied, focused and peaceful in their day to day living.

In summation to the initial question, we are here to witness. We are here to observe. We are here to rediscover and remember who we are.

We *are* infinite consciousness. We *are not* the mind.

While one can use the mind to change and transform themselves, the truth about *who we really are can never be changed.*

It was Norman Vincent Peale who coined the term *Infinite Possibilitarian*. It is now time to wake up to the fact that anything is possible in each moment.

As you encounter perceived limitations on your path, know that these illusions are merely there to awaken you. It is in the welcoming of these perceived limitations that one can rediscover a much bigger Universe than they ever dreamed possible.

It is this simple shift in thinking that will expand your consciousness, allowing you to see possibilities in life where once you thought you were stuck.

What you are thinking and feeling (or vibrating) right now has a definite and direct impact on your immediate future.

That having been said, you are *not* your thoughts and you are *not* your feelings, despite the fact that they are an integral part of the physical experience.

To transcend the mind is akin to *watching* your thoughts and feelings pass by, choosing which thought and/or feeling to entertain at any given moment.

Whatever influences the mind also affects the body. All diseases get into the body by way of the mind, courtesy of persistent and continued mental tension and worry. Unfortunately, most are unaware of this profound truth.

In keeping, it has been said that the mind can either be the cause of one's bondage or the cause of one's liberation. Negative thoughts beget bondage. Positive thoughts beget liberation.

While stilling the chatter of the mind can aid in mental and physical relaxation, what is even more important is recognizing and acknowledging that you are *not* your mind.

Transcending the dualistic mind is the battle of surrendering the bullying of the mind (ego dominated existence) to mindfulness (awareness of one's thoughts, actions and motivations).

Mindfulness means *being aware of the moment in which we are living.*

Mindfulness is *meditation in action,* allowing life to unfold without the limitation of prejudgment.

Mindfulness means being open to an awareness whilst becoming that *Infinite Possibilitarian.*

Mindfulness pertains to existing in a *relaxed state of attentiveness*, one that involves both the inner world of thoughts and feelings, as well as the outer world of actions and perceptions.

Choosing at least one activity each day, to carry out in a mindful manner (giving it your full attention), helps considerably.

If you are chopping vegetables, take the time to absorb the colors, the textures, the smells, the motions, the tastes.

If you are exercising on a treadmill, take the time to feel your muscles moving as you walk, run, jog, speed up, slow down.

That having been said, one can learn to live the entirety of their day in *mindful* meditation.

There is no witness. There is no judgment. You have succeeded in becoming an observer without engaging the mind. Thoughts and feelings are simply thoughts and feelings. They are not who you are.

Before one can work toward transcending the mind, one must reprogram (reconfigure) the subconscious mind. This is what I had to do in order to eclipse a life filled with total negative media bombardment.

The battlefield of the mind is merely the war that plays out between dark (ego) and light (mindfulness), a battle that everyone must conquer.

Such is the journey towards self-realization, a journey in consciousness, a journey in metamorphosis, the quest for self-transformation, the journey of an observer, the journey to freedom. Such is the evolution of man.

How, then, does one get there?

Everywhere you turn, one can easily read articles and books about the power of the subconscious mind. Like the hard drive on a computer that stores all pertinent computer files, so, too, can one's subconscious mind be compared to such an analogy.

The subconscious is where one locates everything that is not located in one's conscious mind, such as previous life experiences and memories. These are our original files, so to speak.

In order to gain access to this databank of information, in order to make changes to the original files, one must bypass the conscious mind. This, then, allows one to neutralize the negatives of the past (as memories cannot be changed) in order to gain the positives in the now.

Meditation is but one avenue open to the seeker who wishes to upgrade their operating system.

At first, you will hear your own thoughts forming in your mind. You may quickly come to realize that there tends to be much continuous repetition to your thoughts. Herein lies the greatest challenge, for there will be many thoughts that will arise as you are attempting to meditate.

In the very beginning, you will find yourself getting lost in them. Trying to remain unattached to the chatter in your head is the most difficult part.

You merely wish to become an observer, standing at the sidelines, if you will. As soon as you pass judgment on what you are observing, the thoughts will drag you down.

Pretend that you are outside, observing the clouds as they float across the sky. Now imagine your thought forms as the very clouds that are passing you by.

It is in coming to this realization that you can honestly say *I have become a witness to my own mind*.

There may also be pictures and images that begin to filter through. Try to become a witness to these visualizations as well.

Do not engage with either the thoughts or the images. Simply accept them while remaining unattached. Do not judge them. Remember, you are merely the observer.

You may also notice your body responding (emotional reactions) to specific thought forms that are filtering through. Once again, you must step out of the emotion.

One should not allow an emotion to control them while in the physical body. You are merely the observer. You may continue to be the witness, but only without judgment.

Even though *becoming a witness* to thought forms, pictures, images and emotions, is not an easy task, it is something that *needs to be practiced every day*.

As you are able to experience success with this while in a meditative state, so, too, shall you be able to practice living a *waking meditation* throughout your entire day.

While it is imperative that you become aware of what goes on in your mind when you are going about your daily life, it is important that you continue to step back, thereby maintaining the stance of an objective observer.

When you are able to experience this with considerable success, you can say that you are practicing a mindfulness type of meditation.

It is also important to realize that there is a monumental difference between you (as the observer) and the things that are observed by you.

As you become more of a witness to your own mind, your consciousness is becoming more aware of itself.

What this means is that the egoic mind will begin to become quiet so that you can learn to reside, in a pure and nonjudgmental way, in what can be called the real Self.

All of the varied forms of meditation have but one purpose: to introduce you to the experiencing of consciousness. With this, then, comes the realization that this is all there is.

As you dedicate yourself to this practice, on an intense and daily basis, you will begin to observe transformation on many levels, each as unique as the individual.

In addition to meditation, affirmations and visualizations can also be used as a transformational tool, a way of bypassing the conscious mind.

Affirmations are personal statements written in both positive and present tense terms. The more emotion one evokes upon saying these affirmations aloud, the more powerful they become.

Affirmations are positive statements, or directions, you make to yourself in order to bring about changes in your subconscious behavior patterns to whatever you will them to be.

For affirmations to be effective, they must always be stated as positive, already accomplished, results.

Wording them in futuristic terms, such as [1] **I will be**, [2] **I am going to be**, or [3] **I would like to be** actually *prevents the changes from ever taking place* because we are always in the now.

Therefore, *giving energy to the positive trait*, such as **I am always Unselfishly Loving** *always supersedes the negative*, (as in **I will become Unselfishly Loving**).

You need to *feel*, *mean* and *believe* the words as you say them, or the affirmation will not be an effective tool.

When it comes to visualization, yet another medium, I find it incredibly difficult to see the pictures while also trying to put myself in the image. It is quite difficult to get emotionally excited about a specific impression when all my mind sees are some dark and fuzzy attempts at a new reality.

Now that I have discovered Mind Movies,[1] an absolutely phenomenal metaphysical tool, I am able to visualize with increasing clarity. Mind Movies is a *multi-media tool* that allows you to create a vision of what you want, scored with your favorite song; the one that makes you feel good, the one that makes you want to dance, the one that makes you smile and sing along.

Freedom experienced on an inner level is the very freedom that all seek, for it is the *real freedom*. This is what you experience when you are able to still the mind.

A calm mind is a powerful mind.

Peace, contentment, happiness and bliss are to be found when one experiences this silence, this stillness, this sense of calm.

Accordingly, there are also additional benefits.

You will find that your ability to concentrate improves.

You will find that you have more patience, showing more tact in responding to difficult situations.

---

[1] http://www.mindmovies.com/?10107

You will find that others do not hold as much sway over you (what they think of you and say about you) as before.

You will find yourself responding to situations with less anxiety and worry.

As difficulties arise, you will demonstrate an increased ability to maintain a sense of inner poise and common sense.

You will find that you are sleeping better.

In addition, all of the above vastly improves your ability to meditate.

Inner peace enables one to feel grounded, to feel balanced. In these stressful times, this is what is needed by all.

Developing the inner ability to still the mind (through such tools as meditation, detachment, visualizations, affirmations and yoga) will take you a considerable distance towards both attaining *and* maintaining inner balance and peace of mind.

There are many who will argue that, based on the degree of evil that exists in the world, God simply does not exist. They say that if the world was created by God, the perfect Creator, then it would have been perfect. As it stands, the world is not perfect, thereby establishing the imperfection of its Creator; ergo, there is no God.

Theism, in its broadest sense, is the belief that at least one deity exists. On a more specific note, theism revolves around the belief in a monotheistic God (which takes us back to Akhenaton) and his relationship to the Universe.

Agnosticism refers to the viewpoint that religious claims, metaphysical claims, and deity existence claims, are unknown.

Atheism is commonly described as the position that there are no deities in existence (due to a lack of empirical data).

I do not view Creation as a haphazard event, nor do I view life as meaningless. This, however, is my truth.

The Universe is a finite, conscious being. In having spoken about energy and matter, science tells us that neither can be destroyed.

The worshipping of gods and goddesses is something that has existed for many millennia.

It is my belief that God/dess is truth. In addition, truth is the good in all people, both individually and collectively.

Writing is something that fulfills my personal truth. In expressing this truth, am I also not expressing God/dess?

With God/dess being expressed through my physical being, am I also not expressing the infinite intelligent source which sustains All That Is?

As truth is my inspiration, is not God/dess also my inspiration?

If we believe that the macrocosm is the microcosm, would not trying to prove the physical existence of God/dess also equate to trying to prove the physical existence of our very selves?

For everything that is created, there is something that creates.

God/dess creates.

We create.

Ego is the instrument of personality and choice, meaning that we get to experience life, time and again, from a multitude of options. Choices are made, courtesy of each incarnation.

While all choices seem to originate out of the truth being experienced on an individual level, one demonstrates God/dess when they are able to become *unlimited* in their truth(s).

Truth is always ongoing, evolving, being created every moment. Truth is created by every thought that you have.

There is a paradox associated with truth. When you come to understand that *everything* is true and yet *nothing* is true, that is when you shall be able to see that just as you perceive truth to be that which you determine it to be, so may all.

In continuation of this explanation, in the moment that you no longer give credence to a truth, it is no longer real, for you have since moved to a new truth.

When you come to understand that truth *is* and *can be* all things, then you are free, no longer enslaved to laws, rules, dogma or intellectual understanding, as is also the case in attempting to prove and/or disprove the conclusiveness of God/dess.

You learn to become *multi-faceted in your truth*, meaning that you are not *one* truth, but *all* truths.

As you come into your own alignment with truth, you, too, shall denote that anything that does not serve you, anything that is not in resonance with your inner truth, shall fall away.

While all things are derived from thought, which is God/dess, it is equally important to realize that God/dess is not simply one formulated thought, but the reality of *all* thoughts.

This means that individual truths, as held by you, as held by me, *are all true*, for each expresses the truth(s) of their experience at any given moment in time.

While there is truth in all things, so, too, is there *refinement* in all things. In fact, each moment serves to refine truth, which is why *God/dess is not a state of perfection*, but rather *a state of becoming*.

In embracing the diversity of life, with quiet acceptance and without judgment, one acknowledges that everything is the way that it is due to the individual and/or collective choices that have been made.

Given that we are creators, orchestrating our lives based on free will, one comes to endorse that there is much greatness at work on this planet. This is what allowed the noted sages of the past to remain at peace in the face of monumental challenge.

Therein lies *my* conclusiveness, the conclusiveness that I was able to find within.

We have all experienced and lived the ego. "The great enlightenment traditions have long spoken about the "enemy within" and about uprooting the need to cling to a false and separate sense of self. Their teachings encourage us to tame, transcend and purify, or in some cases slay, this pernicious foe of the spiritual heart." [2]

It appears, however, that psychologists define ego from a different perspective, claiming it to be "the command center of the psyche without which we could not function. Not only is the ego essential in human development ... it is responsible for creating and sustaining the very civilization on which all of our lives depend." [3]

This editorial, then, as written by Andrew Cohen, puts forth a very important question.

What is the spiritual seeker to make of these two seemingly contradictory definitions?

---

[2] EnlightenNext Magazine (2008). *What Is Ego? Friend or Foe.* Retrieved April 30, 2010 at http://www.wie.org/j17/editorial.asp
[3] Ibid.

Most definitely a question to ponder, especially when "therapists tell us to develop the self" while the "Buddhists say there is no self." [4] How is that for total confusion? Taking it one step further, "psychologists explain how the ego is created" as compared with religions explaining "how the ego is transcended." [5] Go figure.

Andrew Cohen, the publisher of EnlightenNext Magazine, has been dubbed the twenty-first century spiritual teacher and pioneer of evolutionary enlightenment.

He has come to understand that "the way in which we understand and relate to the ego has everything to do with the way in which we understand and relate to all life, *including* spiritual enlightenment." [6]

Cohen shares further insight into the two different parts of the self.

The Authentic Self is passionately interested in dynamic evolution. The Ego, by comparison, is deeply invested in its own narcissistic fears and desires (the one and only obstacle to spiritual enlightenment).

---

[4] EnlightenNext Magazine (2008). *What Is Ego? Friend or Foe.* Retrieved April 30, 2010 at http://www.wie.org/j17/editorial.asp
[5] Ibid.
[6] Ibid.

One *cannot* be filled with, and directed by, both darkness and light at the same time. There is a choice that must be made, with one of these facets taking over the helm of the mind.

Negative feelings, negative thoughts and negative emotions are like toxins that, if suppressed and/or held onto for long periods of time, will manifest in physical form. This is why it is so important to learn how to release negativity. Learning how to change negative self talk into positive self talk takes time, especially considering that we are only *consciously aware* of about 10% of the thoughts that buzz about in our heads.

For many years, too numerous to count, I found myself existing in a state of worry, stress, fear and guilt, both at home and in the workplace. Watching the news on the television kept me in a controlled state of restless anxiety.

I had no idea that the media was so biased in their news coverage, that it was their job to saturate us, to have everyone view the same news, thereby orchestrating all of us to respond in the same manner.

This meant that there was a great propensity for millions and millions of people to broadcast similarly negative responses (vibrations).

Like a sponge, when surrounded by other negative minded people, I would sink deeper and deeper into altering depressive states. I was being controlled by that voice in my head. It was almost impossible to achieve and maintain a positive outlook on life when my mindset was governed by such negativity.

As soon as I became aware that my thoughts, my words and my actions were energy based, I knew that I had no choice but to work towards reconfiguring the wiring of my brain.

I had to learn to think and respond from a more positive outlook. I was no longer willing to allow my ego to reign supreme. This was *a stance that took considerable time and monumental effort.*

How does one begin to go about understanding how they think?

How does one begin to examine, without criticism, the belief system(s) that they are privy to?

The easiest way to start is by *observing your actions and reactions* to people, to things, to situations.

As much as possible, you need to detach yourself from your subjective responses.

Remain as objective as is possible, under the circumstances of the time (and it *does* get easier), for your primary goal is to understand *why* you think the thoughts that you do and *why* you respond to people and situations in a specific way.

Once you begin *questioning your programmed* beliefs and ideas, you need to be ready to *replace them* with beliefs and ideas that resonate with you. In so doing, you begin to embark on an internal and personal mental shift.

Do not be afraid to seek the answers to the questions that every individual, at some time, will ask of themselves.

Who am I?

Why am I here?

What is my purpose?

What is reality?

Do not be afraid to question the information that comes to you.

This is an important part of the process.

As you begin questioning, thereby experiencing this necessary internal shift, your energy signature, your vibration, changes. You will find yourself, more and more, aligning with a higher consciousness. This is what is meant by the *thinning of the veil*.

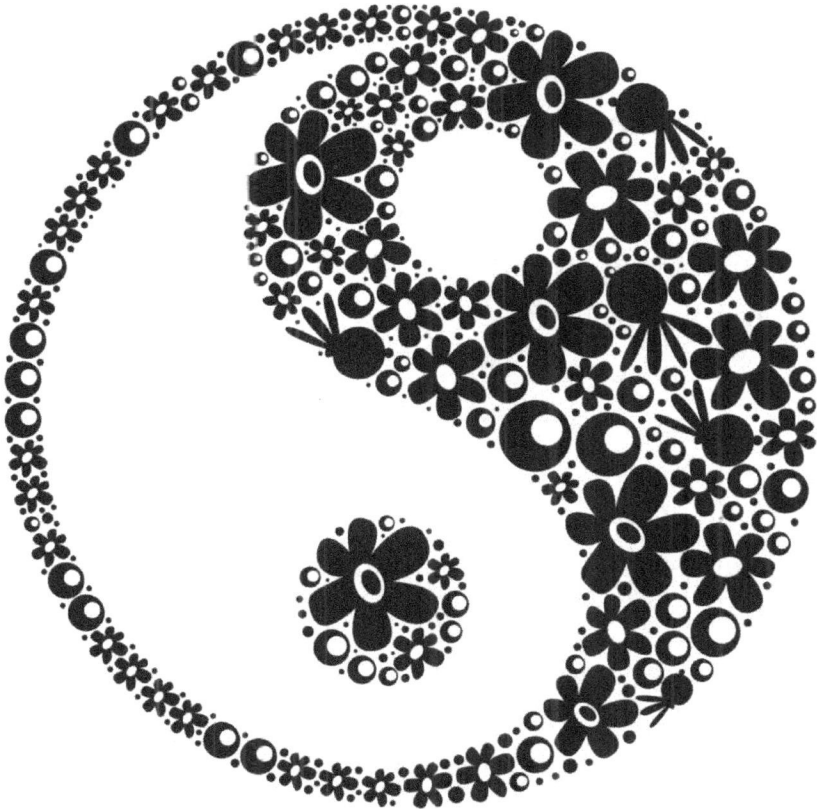

The Challenges We Face

According to Rumi ... *No opposite can be known without its opposite. If duality did not exist, how would we know enough to yearn and strive for wholeness, for completion, for unity?*

There is much truth to these very words.

There appears to exist a duality in this wondrous Cosmos of ours, an inevitable existence of interconnected opposites: male and female, Yin and Yang, good and evil, day and night, life and death, happiness and sadness, new and old, spirit and body, same and different.

Such is the natural law that appears to govern the whole of creation and life as we know it, and yet there are proponents who claim that duality means believing that we are alone, that we are isolated from others, that we are separate from All That Is.

It is my belief that all is connected, that all is one. In remembering our divine nature, we are both the whole and the parts of the whole; the interconnected totality of all life.

Such is where duality begins to blur, changing to nonduality. This is where we begin to comprehend that we must strive to find the oneness, the unconditional love, the peace of mind, that exists beyond the duality of our experience.

Nonduality lets us see that all is connected, that all is unified. In realizing that we share a oneness, we come to terms with the fact that we are no longer separate. All that exists is in the here and now.

The next question becomes how do we get from where we currently find ourselves to where it is that we want to be?

Jerry Katz, the author of *One: Essential Writings on Nonduality*, says that "if you have ever had a sense of "something" deeper and more meaningful that lies beyond the everyday you, yet that is you in some way, you have had a taste of nonduality. The taste of nonduality is the sense of unity, peace, "something" vaster than the everyday you." [7]

In continuation, "if you have ever felt deeply dissatisfied, intensely unhappy, psychically imprisoned, it might be said that you can only feel this dissatisfaction because part of you

---

[7] Katz, Jerry. *Nonduality*. Retrieved April 27, 2008 from http://nonduality.net/

knows there is a place of freedom. That freedom is the experience of nonduality." [8]

What Katz shared next certainly resonated deep within my soul.

"After experiencing the taste of nonduality, you may begin to *pursue* nonduality [through such mediums as books, crystals, meditation, teachers, spiritual practices, retreats] and since you are not separate from the "something" that is deeper, vaster, more meaningful than the everyday you, it follows that this pursuit is the *discovery of who you really are.*" [9]

It is now clear to me that nonduality refers to an exploration of oneness, the fundamental quality of everything that exists. The challenge, herein, lies in the fact that *things can appear different without being separate.*

Whilst I am learning that I am no stranger to nonduality, a word that means not two, given that this *is* my very pursuit as well, I would certainly never lay claim to being an expert in this area either.

---

[8] Katz, Jerry. *Nonduality.* Retrieved April 27, 2008 from http://nonduality.net/
[9] Ibid.

While learning to love yourself is not always an easy task, it certainly is not an impossibility.

You may need to hear what others love about you in order to come to acknowledge that you *have many things* to love about yourself.

Even if you find it hard to believe that someone could like a particular thing about you, it is important to trust that your friends know, and can identify, what it is that they like about you.

If you keep hearing those critical voices inside your head, make a list of everything that you like about yourself, being as honest as you can. If you are having trouble establishing a list, take the time to think about what you value and love about your friends. Do you also exhibit the same?

Take the time to say something positive about yourself. It could be something that you like about yourself. It could be something that you did to make yourself feel good. It could be something that you did to make someone else feel good.

Be sure to look at yourself in the mirror and say the words with truthful feeling.

Every time someone tells you something about yourself that makes you feel good, write it down so that you can revisit it later. Put these slips of paper in a special place, reading them as often as the need arises.

If you come from a dysfunctional family, it is important to realize that you did nothing wrong. If you are the survivor of abuse, it is important to realize that you did nothing wrong. Clearly, having survived such immense difficulties, you have the inner courage and strength to love yourself, even if you are doubtful. Carrying a piece of tumbled Rose Quartz will help you connect with your inner child.

While it may sound silly, some people have tremendous success with affirmations. Take the time to write out strong and loving messages to yourself, putting them in places where you will see them. You must also remember to read them.

If you *believe* and *feel* the truth in what you are stating about yourself, affirmations can be a magnificent tool to work with. Be sure to take the time to read the affirmation slowly so that you can perceive the power and emotion behind the words.

Take the time to do things for yourself that make you feel sensational.

A favorite tool of mine is <u>The Power Word Cards</u> [10] deck as produced by Onwords & Upwards, a company based in British Columbia, Canada. These unique, inspiring and practical cards contain sixty empowering words with definitions and three sample affirmations per word.

Power words are carefully chosen words which, with conscious use, can empower you to live a more fulfilling life. You can play with these cards to help you build an empowering vocabulary, create your own personal affirmations, stay focused and inspired every day, and have fun with family and friends.

Your everyday words can become powerful, creative words by how you consciously choose to use them in your daily expression. The Power Word Cards help you focus attention on the importance of the words you think and speak and on their power to create your heart's desire.

In summation, when we love ourselves, we are happier.

---

[10] http://www.onwordsupwords.com/onwords2.html

I have *not* come to be anyone's savior. I am my own savior. In turn, you, too, have come to save yourself.

I have *not* come to create a religion. I have *not* come to be labeled a guru. I am my own guru. You, too, are your own guru, whether you believe it or not.

I *have* come to demonstrate love.

I *have* come to demonstrate acceptance of all.

I *have* come to demonstrate reverence for all life.

We are all connected. Together, we share a vast oneness. Nothing is separate. This is merely the illusion that was created; the very illusion that has been used, by many, to create a monopoly of wealth and power. After 2,000 years of such infiltration as we know it, *we are here to remember who we are.*

One of the most challenging tasks we face is to learn to become nonjudgmental.

As you learn to let things be, disentangling from both emotionally charged situations as well as from the collective intellectual mindset of laws, rules and dogma, you are able to experience your own freedom and resolution.

Do not try to restrict others by judging them, controlling them, or blaming them, for this limits your understanding of them. By direct association, this behavior also serves to limit their understanding of themselves.

Just as you have experienced yours, so, too, must you allow others the time and opportunity to experience their own freedom, their own resolution, moving forward as best they know how.

Whenever you judge people or situations, you envelop them within your own belief system. In this way, you blind yourself to the truth about them, forgetting that they, too, are whole and divine.

When you respond to people with love and compassion, you readily move from conflict to harmony. Such is the very freedom sought by all

When you remember, embrace and share your divinity, you free others to walk their truth. You become accepting of their truth, for such is whom they are.

Become who and what you truly are by *listening to the God within you.* Become who and what you truly are by both knowing and accepting that *God speaks through feelings*, for they will be your guide to truth, further directing you on your individual path of enlightenment.

Compassion is who we are.

The keys to compassion lie in *your ability to embrace all experiences* as part of the one, without judgment.

This is the greatest challenge that all must face as they move towards greater states of personal mastery, which is the return to your truest form.

Demonstrating love through compassionate allowing means that you must love others enough to *allow the range* of their experience.

Compassion is what you *allow yourself to Become.*

Compassion is your birthright.

Compassion is your *truest nature.*

Compassion allows you to view from an equal standpoint.

There is no judgment.

Mastery of compassion means redefining what your world means to you. It is *not* about forcing change upon the world around you.

You, and only you, choose *how* you respond.

As a being of compassion, you are offered the opportunity to *transcend polarity while still living within the polarity*. This is what enables you to move forward with life, a life filled with freedom, resolution and peace.

Compassion means *living in trust*.

Compassion means *living with joy*.

What we do and what we think are key in creating our world.

Living a new truth must first start with the individual. You must have *the wisdom and the courage* to embrace this new life, this new truth, as your reality.

We are part of a much larger Galactic family than we have ever believed possible.

Truth Alignment

I have never claimed to be anyone other than who I AM in this particular incarnation. While I believe that I have lived countless lifetimes, with emotions and feelings and experiences gleaned from each, all serving to make me who I AM at this very moment, I have no recollection of who I may have been outside of this current drama. All that I know, with absolute certainty, is that I am here to experience the now.

I know that research, reading and writing are my passion. I love being able to create with words, to play with words, to experiment with words, to orchestrate with words.

I am deeply appreciative of the experience(s) that we create for our own learning. I find that I am able to take great satisfaction in understanding who I am Becoming.

The only truths that I can fully embrace are the concepts of change, as followed by truth.

I am here as both teacher and student. Indeed, such can be said about each and every individual.

Veracity At Its Best

I love how the synchroncities of this vast and awesome Universe continue to keep me sitting on the edge of my seat, only to anticipate (expect) more of the same.

While I have not yet become adept at meditation, I do take the time to practice *mindful* living in the now.

While I used to shy away from my eccentricity, I now embrace it wholeheartedly.

While there may be many who think me strange, given the spiritual and metaphysical beliefs that I hold as my truths in this moment, I am deeply appreciative of the freedom that comes with thinking outside of the box.

I hold true to myself.

I take the time to listen to my inner soul, to commune with my intuition.

I do my utmost to think with my heart as compared to my head.

I strive, always, to speak from the heart.

I feel with my heart.

In speaking about my own personal experiences, it has been in the *giving of myself* to others that I have felt ......

the most spiritual, the most consciously aware, the most empowered, the most fruitful, the most uplifted, the most expansive, the most virtuous, the most energetic, the most positive, the most true.

You, too, are here to experience and remember the same.

Should you choose to accept, *living your truth is the mission that you have been entrusted with.*

Mankind is awakening into a new era.

"The Human Mind is the vehicle in which consciousness enters into and experiences creation. One aspect of the mind is Thought … the other is Imagination, which is its natural evolution. Thought and Imagination are two sides of the same coin." [11]

Knowing that our world is an expression of our human imagination, might it be that we can come to understand thought enough to create something new and wonderful for ourselves?

Imagination allows one to live in the "freedom of limitless possibility, for all things in this world are imagination of which consciousness is the animating power in a world of

---

[11] *Universal Laws* article located on the Imagination Awakened Ministry website. Retrieved May 4, 2010 from http://www.i-am.cc/us/Ministry.htm

shadows. It has been said that God is in all things." [12]   This means that both thought and imagination are also God, does it not?

One attracts what they believe to be true.

This is why it is so important to become aware of your unconscious programming, your unconscious patterns. In so doing, you open yourself up to becoming even more aware of the world around you.

As you become more aware of the world that exists within, you are on your way to being freed from the egoic mind.

---

[12] *Universal Laws* article located on the Imagination Awakened Ministry website. Retrieved May 4, 2010 from http://www.i-am.cc/us/Ministry.htm

Too often we affirm the negative, over and over again, in our daily lives without even realizing that we are only attracting more and more of the very same into our lives.

Interestingly enough, if we give our attention (attraction) to something while also *emphatically* stating **I do not want this in my life**, we are *still attracting what we do not want* because we are continuing to give our attention to that which we do not want.

As a result, this can actually railroad all of the positively inspired thoughts and aspirations that we are doing our best to advance towards.

It is only when we *no longer give any attention* to that which we do not want that we can actually start attracting more of what we do want. This is chiefly due to the fact that we are better able to remain focused on what we want.

I know this sounds complicated, and that you may end up rereading this introduction more than once, but it need not be.

As soon as you start attracting more of what you *do want* in your life, you will begin to experience a sense of complete freedom.

Freedom has *nothing* to do with the outside world and *everything* to do with what dwells on the inside.

How can this be, you ask?

We are creating our own experience(s) of life with both our thoughts as well as the way in which we process the world around us.

All is vibration; so, too, are we vibrational beings living in a vibrational Universe.

The thoughts that we think emit a vibration.

The words we speak emit a vibration.

The actions we engage in emit a vibration.

Many do not yet understand that they create their own reality via thoughts, feelings, emotions, words and actions. In this light, many are creating by default, albeit unconsciously.

It is only when you become *consciously aware* of your thoughts, feelings, emotions, words and actions that you can learn to become a *deliberate* creator, choosing only that which you *want to create more of* in your life.

It is through your attention, your wanting, your desire and your emotion that you ask of the Universe. While we need not ask in the form of words, one must always *feel* the emotions attached to that which they desire.

Thoughts act like radio waves or radio signals. If there is something that you want, you need to place your attention (focus) on it. By virtue of the Law of Attraction, it *will* come to you. That having been said, one should always be careful what they ask for (by way of their attention and their focus).

Having the desire for something is clearly not enough, but it is a valid starting point. You also have to *achieve vibrational harmony with your desire*. This means that you must learn to *feel the thought into fruition*.

Feel it. Feel what it is like to have acquired it. Feel the enjoyment of having it. Imagine already having attained it.

The more attention and feeling you give to your thought (your desire), the more impetus, the more energy, the more push, it has behind it.

You will know when you have achieved vibrational harmony with your thought(s) and desire(s) by virtue of the way that you feel.

You will be feeling joyous, happy, excited, energized, exuberant, spirited, upbeat, jolly, contented, chipper, elated, gratified, lively, on cloud nine, peaceful, thrilled and sunny, just to provide you with differing word comparisons.

You must first come to understand that *you get what you think about*. Remember, all is energy.

Another exceptionally important part of this manifestation equation comes to light when you become *aware of what you are thinking* because *this is when you begin to realize* that you are in *total and absolute control of your own experience*, no matter the circumstances.

Everything comes down to the power of intent.

You always get what you ask for. You always get what you think about. You always get what you become focused on.

In this light, one can actually say that prayers are always heard and always answered, be it of a positive frequency (where you feel exhilaration and anticipation) or a negative frequency (where you feel depressed, angry, disappointed).

This is why it becomes imperative that you become *aware* of what it is that you are actually putting out there in terms of vibration.

The more you focus on any given thought, the more you are living the vibration of that thought. The stronger your vibrational alignment (harmony) becomes, the faster you are able to manifest that thought.

This is truly empowering. It is also very humbling in its illumination.

It is through the focus of your own consciousness that you can learn to manipulate the energy that is used to create worlds. This, too, was both known and practiced by the ancients.

What you think and what you get are *always* a vibrational match.

You, alone, hold the key to creating that which you desire.

Do you wish to create by default, meaning that you are not aware of what it is that you are creating for yourselves, and yet you continue to create anyway?

Do you wish to create on a total conscious level, meaning that you become a deliberate creator, knowing exactly what you want to create in your life?

These are the very questions that need to be asked.

When you are completely focused on your desire *and* when you know that your desire shall come to be, that is when you have created a belief.

As a creator, you must *believe* in your creation. Likewise, as a creator, you must also *believe* in yourself as a creator.

There exists a very strong correlation between what you are thinking, what you are feeling, and what you are receiving. It cannot be put any more succinctly than that.

If you are in constant alignment with your inner being, with who you really are, you are following your bliss, as per Joseph Campbell.

Do you wish to continue to observe things as they currently exist in your life? If your answer is yes, then you shall continue to create by default (an unconscious act of creation).

Do you wish to imagine things as you want them to be? If your answer is yes, then you are already on your way to becoming a deliberate creator (a conscious act of creation).

So, then, how does one become a deliberate creator?

First off, you begin by *deciding what you want.*

You must be *very clear* about what this is. You have to *know what you want.* You have to *feel what you want.*

The good thing about knowing what you want is that you also know what you do not want. Therein lies the necessary dichotomy.

You also have to realize that while you are a creator, so, too, is everyone else on this planet. In summation, this actually means that we are all partners in co-creation, does it not?

What a powerful statement.

Take some time to ponder what has just been shared, for therein lies the diversity that exists, the diversity of creation. This diversity is also what *helps you determine* that which you want.

You are here to create your own experiences. You are *not* here to control the creation(s) of another.

Just because your choice and their choice may differ, such does not make you right and them wrong, or vice versa.

In my novel, *A Travel in Time to Grand Pré*, I refer to this as *compassionate allowing*.

Shaped by our thoughts, we become what we think. Simply put, and as already previously discussed, "what you think about is where your energy goes. Put another way, energy moves to whatever your consciousness focuses on." [13]

I am a firm believer in maintaining my own power. That having been said, I am responsible for whatever I have created.

Being responsible also means that I have to watch what I think and watch what I say, all in an effort to make sure that I never, intentionally, give my power away.

There are but two choices, meaning that one can either maintain conscious control or unconscious control over their life.

It becomes my choice to choose the former, just as it becomes your choice to also choose for yourself.

---

[13] Sharp, Michael. (2004) *Dossier of The Ascension: A Practical Guide to Kundalini Activation* (p. 60). St. Albert, AB: Avatar Publications.

While many people have very little understanding of the power that they wield (or not, should that also be their choice), it is true that "the more you are interested in something, the more you think about it, and the more you focus intent on it, the *closer you are* to that thing. The less you think about something and the less you focus, then the farther you are away from it." [14]

Essentially, this means that being the creator of your life, you can manifest something into physicality, into matter, with continued and concentrated effort, because energy always follows intent.

Buddha understood the universal law that dictates the following – *we are shaped by our thoughts* – thereby becoming what we think.

While you may not yet accept such a law, such comes into being, courtesy of your beliefs, your feelings, your thoughts.

It also needs to be stated that we are also the creators of our own misery in that whatever we do, we do to ourselves, be it by way of thoughts, feelings, intentions or actions.

---

[14] Sharp, Michael. (2004) *Dossier of The Ascension: A Practical Guide to Kundalini Activation* (p. 63). St. Albert, AB: Avatar Publications.

While this should offer compelling spiritual reflection, most imperative for self examination, such is not always the case.

Beliefs have a dominant and powerful effect on every aspect of one's life.

There have been individuals and powerful institutions, throughout history, all willing to kill for their beliefs. It becomes even more shocking, in the 21st century, to realize that this mentality still exists.

It is for this very reason that every individual must be *willing to scrutinize* the very beliefs that they hold dear, for the simple reason that one's beliefs serve to create their lives.

There are very important questions that need to be asked.

Do my beliefs, thoughts, feelings, intentions and actions *prevent* the manifestation of unselfish love?

Do my beliefs, thoughts, feelings, intentions and actions *allow* the manifestation of unselfish love?

Do my beliefs, thoughts, feelings, intentions and actions *give rise* to anger, hatred and harm?

Do my beliefs, thoughts, feelings, intentions and actions *bring forth* tranquility, love and healing?

Do my beliefs, thoughts, feelings, intentions and actions *make for an improved world* for all, myself included?

Do my beliefs, thoughts, feelings, intentions and actions *make for an abominable world* for others, myself included?

We live in a world that has long created the illusion of separateness from the Universal Spirit. It has been this very *illusion of separateness* that led to the creation of *selfishness*.

I personally see this as being a very exciting time. In knowing that we create our own reality by the very thoughts that we think, the very words that we verbalize, the very actions that we employ, *now is the time* to learn to let go of fear so that one can concentrate solely on the expansion of love and forgiveness.

We are here to heal ourselves of this very affliction.

In working with thought forms, it is imperative that one stay positive. It is only in thinking positive thoughts that we continue to attract more positive people, as well as positive events and happenings, into our lives.

In this way we become ripples in a pond, creating a domino effect of increased positivity out into the world.

On the flipside, of course, the more we focus on the negative, the depressed, the dismal, the more negativity we bring into our lives. Clearly, we must become more aware of our thoughts in order to eliminate the unnecessary and judgmental ones.

It is for this very reason that I no longer watch the news on television, read magazines, read newspapers, or listen to the news on the radio. I made the decision to eliminate all media negativity in my life for the simple reason that I found myself existing in a state of depression, unable to focus on the joys associated with life and living.

There is a way to manage a better sleep at night: stop watching the news before going to bed.

In keeping with the changes that we are trying to bring forth within, it is important to remember that for every action or non-action, there is a consequence. When we give our minds and our responsibility away, we give our lives away.

Do you really want to keep living this way? It is important to remember that most of the media is controlled by a few. Take the time to use discernment. Look for the hidden agenda.

The following bullets, as paraphrased from the work of David Icke, are of monumental importance.

- Why is this information being presented to you?

- What is their *real* agenda?

- Is it a case of problem – reaction – solution, meaning that *they* create a problem so that we react as they intend, thereby asking for a fix?

- Do *they*, then, offer a solution?

- Might this *solution* be what *they* really wanted in the first place?

The real power lies with the multitude. Do not allow yourself to be fooled. Infinite power exists within every single individual, yourself included.

We have the power to decide our own destiny, but only if we do not give that power away.

When something happens that we do not like, why is it that we have a tendency to look for someone else to blame?

When there is a problem in the world, why is it that we have a tendency to wonder what *they* are going to do about it?

In retrospect, it is this very non-action type of response that has resulted in the giving away of our power.

The same institutions and organizations that control the world on a global level want to control your mind because when they have succeeded in doing this (when you are no longer thinking for yourself), they have you where they want you; hence, the answer lies in taking our minds back, thinking for ourselves, questioning what we are being told in an attempt to redefine our own truth(s), while also allowing others to do the same, without judgment or ridicule.

We create our own reality by our thoughts and our actions. If we change both of these, we will begin to change the world, beginning with ourselves, first and foremost. It really is that simple.

More people are waking up to the fact that, in making these necessary and needed thought changes, they are allowing their own frequencies to assist others in this much needed planetary change.

As already touched upon throughout the text, everyone lives in the world of his or her thoughts. Thoughts are energy; hence, positive thoughts attract positive results, naturally, while negative thoughts attract negative results.

Like always attracts like.

Interestingly, body parts, including cells and organs, also have *vibratory signatures*, be they healthy or diseased.

From a scientific standpoint, we also have the power to alter the vibratory signature of our body through thought forms.

Our thoughts, beliefs, expectations, words and actions find their way to the electromagnetic field (aura) which surrounds us.

It is courtesy of this magnetic field, or vibratory signature, that we attract people and situations that match our energy vibration.

We attract those things in our lives (money, relationships, employment, to name just a few) that we focus on. If your mind (thought) is negating the positive, you end up attracting more of what you do not want.

When we focus on having less, that is exactly what we create for ourselves. This is why it becomes imperative to *know* what you want. Monitor your thoughts as carefully as you can, being sure to *think only about what you want*.

Make what you want your burning desire, your major purpose, for these will be the very thoughts that shall manifest in form.

Remain determined to see them fully realized, while doing your utmost to work towards achieving them, even if in small steps. Success comes to those who possess success consciousness.

You get what you think about. You get what you focus on. You get what you talk about. You get what you believe.

To become peace in action, one must be peace.

To become love in action, one must be love.

To become forgiveness in action, one must be forgiveness.

That having been said, continue to do your utmost to keep those thoughts positive.

Gratitude is demonstrated as thankfulness or appreciation. Not only is it a feeling, it is also a state of being. It becomes an attitude to live by.

Gratefulness is also key to living a happy life. Happiness, then, becomes a *spiritual* experience, unlocking the fullness of life, thereby creating a vision for tomorrow.

Remembering that what you focus on expands, the more you focus on the goodness of your life, the more goodness you create for yourself. Every day, give thanks for that which presents itself.

As energy, as vibration, an attitude of gratitude is one of acceptance and harmony. There is no judgment. It is this very vibrational resonance that attracts to you the events, conditions and circumstances, that you desire.

While there may be times when it becomes very difficult to express gratitude, it is during these conflicting times that we have to dig deeper. If one is completely honest, they will come to understand that *all things work for the greater good*, even if this greater good is not immediately forthright.

While it may take some time to acknowledge that what has happened was for their greater good, this, then, allows them to remain in a state of gratitude, no matter how disappointing the initial outcome.

In the words of John F. Kennedy ... *As we express our gratitude, we must never forget that the highest appreciation is not to utter words, but to live by them.*

Due to the fact that most of humanity identifies fully with the ego, believing that this is who they really are, releasing one's self from the egoic mind is a difficult task. The most daunting challenge that we have to face is this: we are *not* our thoughts and emotions.

Although I am unsure as to where the term egoic mind originated, the name is most apt due to the fact that as long as one identifies with the 'thinker', there is a sense of ego connected to every thought, memory, opinion, viewpoint, interpretation, reaction and emotion.

The function of the egoic mind is to *maintain control*, keeping one prisoner to the linear and logical mind. As the egoic mind surrenders, however, we begin to engage in a more conscious experience.

Once there, much vigilance is initially needed in an attempt to maintain the silence. The more you are able to maintain the silence, the less you experience the loud and incessant chattering of the mind.

Until the egoic mind has dissolved completely, one must continue to remain alert to its subterfuge, whether in one's self and/or others. This is a process that has taken me years. It is also a process that I continue to maintain.

If this sounds rather intimidating, it need not be. Humor is a most valuable tool that can be used to short-circuit the spell of the egoic mind.

Upon disengagement of the egoic mind, one is better able to begin to experience, and acknowledge, authentic power as being completely different from ego based power. I quickly came to realize that I was here to be of service (my family, my students, my friends, Mother Earth), but without taking away from myself.

Edgar Cayce actually likens the death of the ego to "the symbology behind the crucifixion of Christ." [15]

The best thing that we can do to save the world is to save the world from our own righteousness as "it is our *righteousness egoic mind* which makes us see problems. In Truth, the only problem is the prevailing mentality that problems do exist and our projection of them into each other and the world.

---

[15] Williams, Kevin. (2006) *Edgar Cayce on Human Origins* article. Retrieved May 7, 2010 from http://www.near-death.com/experiences/cayce03.html

This is actually the most essential message spiritual masters and enlightenment teachers have been sharing with us throughout the ages." [16]

What Nebot shares next is very important, so we all need to sit up and take notice. "By being conscious of our triggers, reactions, and projections, we can transcend them. As we transform, our world transforms. So before becoming an activist to fight for whatever cause you consider noble, consider first that, perhaps, the only thing wrong with the world is your perception of it." [17]

Now *that* paragraph is worth re-reading several times over, especially the last line.

As you "start releasing all the opinions, beliefs, emotions and perceptions that are keeping you separated from others, from this world, and ultimately from God … you will realize that, in Truth, we are all One. You will be blessed with full understanding, acceptance and compassion for everyone and everything. You may still feel inspired to take action, but it won't be motivated by judgment, fear, greed, blame, need, moral obligation or any other egoic energy that motivates

---

[16] Nebot, Jesus. *How to save the world from yourself* article. Retrieved May 7, 2010 from http://www.ru.org/personal-development/how-to-save-the-world-from-yourself.html
[17] Ibid.

most people. Instead, your actions will be inspired by pure, unconditional Love for all that exists. A Divine Love that will take over your life and guide you to selflessly serve other people, animals, nature and the planet at large. Then the world will be saved because you will be saved." [18]

Such clearly leads to the emotional freedom that is sought by each and every being, consciously or unconsciously.

---

[18] Nebot, Jesus. *How to save the world from yourself* article. Retrieved May 7, 2010 from http://www.ru.org/personal-development/how-to-save-the-world-from-yourself.html

Noetic Science refers to the study of human thought. In truth, perfecting one's mind, via their consciousness, is what shall provide us with the emotional freedom that is needed.

The power of the human mind is what the ancient mysteries were all about. In truth, the ancients understood thought more profoundly than we do today. With such knowledge, however, also comes great responsibility.

Lynne McTaggert, author of both *The Field: The Quest For The Secret Force Of The Universe* (2003) as well as *The Intention Experiment: Using Your Thoughts to Change Your Life and the World* (2008), is currently involved with the largest mind over matter experiment in all of human history (or, at least, as we know it), aptly titled The Intention Experiment. This is a global, internet based study, aimed at discovering how human intention, in the forms of distance healing, prayer, group thought and group focus, can change the world.

The basic premise of Noetic Science correlates with the untapped potential of the human mind.

Experiments have shown that human thought, if properly focused, has the ability to affect and change one's physical world on a significant level. Indeed, this is what one may refer to as *mind over matter*.

It is also what has been termed *cosmic consciousness*, meaning that a vast amalgamating of human intention is more than capable of interacting with physical matter. Such can be achieved by way of mass meditation and prayer.

Lynne McTaggart defines cosmic consciousness as being an energy capable of changing the physical world. This energy, while outside the confines of the physical body, is a highly ordered energy.

Focused thought can affect anything. Indeed, human intention, when utilized in this way, can affect the world.

Dr. Masaru Emoto, a creative and visionary Japanese researcher, spent many years studying water, all of which can be viewed in his book, *The Message From Water*.

The human body can range anywhere from 55% to 78% water, depending on physical size. The blood in the body contains almost 70% water. Over 70% of the surface of the planet is covered with water.

In reference to the findings of Dr. Emoto, all of these interrelated components become unequivocally important.

Dr. Emoto was able to provide factual evidence that *human vibrational energy* (in the form of thoughts and words) *is able to affect the molecular structure of water*. With water being the source of all life, its quality and integrity were also noted as being extremely important components.

Dr. Emoto and his fellow colleagues were witness to the reaction of water in keeping with different environmental conditions, including pollution and music.

Their findings have stated that water is alive. We can naturally structure water through the usage of positive and loving emotions, meaning that water is highly responsive to thoughts and words.

The research of Dr. Emoto has provided us with physical evidence that we can *positively heal and transform this planet* by the thoughts that we choose to think and the actions we choose to take in direct association with those thoughts. Such can also be said for ourselves.

The power of intention and prayer appears to influence the water. The higher the purity of the intent, the less of a difference was denoted when distance was an operating variable.

That having been said, *the crystalline structure of the water appears to reflect the composite vibrations* (energy) *being received.*

Lake Biwa, the third oldest lake in the world, sits almost dead center in Japan. A culmination of research involving both Dr. Masaru Emoto and Lynne McTaggart, the first live water Intention Experiment was conducted on Lake Biwa (March 22, 2010). The stated purpose of the experiment was to purify the water of Lake Biwa (which, then, would be demonstrated in reference to the testing of pH water levels).

To read more about this particular Intention Experiment, please visit the following links.

<u>Praying for Water: the results of the Lake Biwa Intention Experiment</u> [19]

<u>The Purifying Effect of Love: the Lake Biwa Intention Experiment, Part 2</u> [20]

---

[19] Retrieved May 11, 2010 at
http://www.theintentionexperiment.com/praying-for-water-the-results-of-the-lake-biwa-intention-experiment.htm
[20] Retrieved May 11, 2010 at
http://www.theintentionexperiment.com/praying-for-water-the-results-of-the-lake-biwa-intention-experiment.htm

It is becoming more clear that human thought can, quite literally, transform one's physical world.

This means that the mind, via the consciousness, has the ability to alter the state of matter. In addition, and perhaps even more importantly, the mind also has the power to encourage the physical world to move in a specific direction.

Does this not mean that we are Masters of our own Universe?

What, then, is it that turns possibility into reality?

Could it actually be that the most essential ingredient in creating our Universe is the *consciousness* that observes it?

As stated previously in the acknowledgments section was a quote attributed to Buddha: *You are what observes, not what you observe.* Quite simply, *we are the consciousness that observes.*

We, as consciousness, have incredible powers. We can heal the world. We can heal ourselves. We can heal our communities. We can make our world exactly as we wish it to be.

Harnessing the true power of the mind, like meditation, requires extensive practice.

That having been said, it does seem to appear that some individuals are more skilled, than others, at manifesting the power of their thoughts.

Is one born with this skill? Might it be affiliated with one's success in a previous incarnation? At this point, the answer seems to be an evading one.

Might this be the missing link between ancient mysticism and the science(s) of today?

Learn deeply of the mind and its mystery for therein lies the true secret of immortality [Bushby, Tony. (2003) The Secret in the Bible, page 6. Queensland, AU: Joshua Books].

There are a number of mystical related works that seem to come to the fore upon further investigation.

I am herein listing but a few that any well intentioned researcher can easily locate.

• *Kybalion*: a study of Hermetic philosophy pertaining to both ancient Egypt and ancient Greece.

• *Zohar*: a collection of Kabbalistic commentaries on the Hebrew Bible (the Torah) designed to guide persons to discover deeper and higher states of spiritual attainment.

- *Bhagavad Gita*: a sacred Hindu scripture of spiritual wisdom from ancient India. Bhagavad means God. Gita means Song. Often called the Song of God, it was Lord Krishna who spoke the Bhagavad Gita.

- The writings of Manly P. Hall.

- Hermetic philosophy

- *Apocrypha*

- *Emerald Tablet of Thoth* (Hermes Trismegistus)

An absolutely wonderful internet resource is the site entitled Internet Sacred Text Archive.[21] Another valuable resource is the Gnostic Society Library. [22]

It seems that man has been on a spiritual quest for many millennia, a quest that pertains to the interconnectedness with all life, a quest that pertains to becoming one with the Universe and everything contained therein.

As forever as this quest has persisted, it has not been an easy one for the greater multitude, given our preprogrammed beliefs. However, change is at hand.

---

[21] http://www.sacred-texts.com/
[22] http://www.gnosis.org/library.html

We are poised on the threshold of a new and wondrous age, an age whereby we are awakening to the need to break free of the old and embrace the new.

What we are finding is that this embracing of the new and seemingly unexplored is not really new at all. Instead, we are simply revisiting that which was once a part of our experience.

Might this be a resurgence of a reverence for the ways of old, the ways of the ancients?

Are we just beginning to realize the validity and authenticity of the ancient and mystical texts?

The search must begin with the wisdom of the ancients.

Learn deeply of the mind and its mystery for therein lies the true secret of immortality [Bushby, Tony. (2003) The Secret in the Bible, page 6. Queensland, AU: Joshua Books].

It is time to rediscover the lost wisdom of the ancients. Your inner knowledge and intuitive consciousness will help pave the way.

Every thought that you perceive has mass. In keeping, it is entirely plausible that a thought can be measured.

Hypothetically speaking, and from a scientific standpoint, the immediate implications become most obvious.

When a thought exerts gravity, that thought can pull things toward it. As already discussed in an earlier chapter, "what you think about is where your energy goes. Put another way, energy moves to whatever your consciousness focuses on." [23]

Truth be told, we just do not think of our thoughts as having mass.

Taking it one step further, let us depart from the individual (or singular) thought form, advancing toward the collective (or plural) thought form.

Having acknowledged what transpires when an individual becomes focused on the manifestation of their own thought(s), what might happen if many people began to focus on the same thought?

This, my friends, is what Noetic Science is all about.

---

[23] Sharp, Michael. (2004). *Dossier of The Ascension: A Practical Guide to Kundalini Activation* (p. 60). St. Albert, AB: Avatar Publications.

As the mass of an individual thought form grows, attracting more of the same, so, too, is it with a collective thought form.

In fact, if enough people were to begin thinking the same thought, such would create a more distinctly measurable effect on our physical world, enabling the thought to manifest with incredible speed.

Within the human mind there lies a secret body of knowledge, a body of knowledge that is alleged to enable its practitioners, meaning ourselves, to access powerful abilities.

Learn deeply of the mind and its mystery for therein lies the true secret of immortality [Bushby, Tony. (2003) The Secret in the Bible, page 6. Queensland, AU: Joshua Books].

Knowledge is power. As one is able to break free of their earthly, preprogrammed, chains, they begin to ascend towards the source of All That Is.

The enlightened sages of yore understood the true power associated with thought and gravitational force.

If we accept, as *Genesis* decrees, that man was created in the image of God, then, so, too, must we also accept that *we were not created inferior* to God; hence, *we are also gods*.

113

The Kingdom of God/dess is located within each and every being living on this wondrous planet. The apostasy lies in the fact that we have been taught it heretical to believe ourselves equal to God.

All For One and One For All, so went the motto (mantra) of the Three Musketeers. The numeral three also immediately brings to mind the trinity. As a name, Trinity brings to mind *The Matrix* movies.

In reference to traditional Christianity, I grew up believing in the trinity: the triune aspect of Father, Son/Daughter and Holy Spirit.

I have since learned to believe in a trinity that consists of spirit, soul and body/personality as outlined by Reverend Simeon Stefanidakis. [24]

My physical body is but a vessel for a most valuable and potent treasure: my mind (consciousness). Truly, we possess abilities of which we are not even aware.

---

[24] Stefanidakis, Rev. Simeon. (2001). *Helping Understand the Mystery of Spirit-Soul-Body* article accessed May 8, 2010 from First Spiritual Temple website located at http://www.fst.org/trinity.htm

Learn deeply of the mind and its mystery for therein lies the true secret of immortality [Bushby, Tony. (2003) <u>The Secret in the Bible</u>, page 6. Queensland, AU: Joshua Books].

The persistent message of man's own divinity (of our hidden potential), very much lies in reference to the mystic, and seemingly cryptic, messages of old.

Know ye not that ye are Gods? were words as spoken by Hermes Trismegistus. In keeping, *Psalm* 82:6 has been attributed to a writer by the name of Asaph. The Hebrew word for gods is Elohim, a word that has also been attributed to angels (*Psalm* 8:5) and human judges (*Exodus* 21:6); hence, the word does not only imply deity. In *John* 10:34, Jesus is quoting Asaph to the unbelieving Jews.

As above, so below is a phrase that has been taken from the Emerald Tablet of Thoth (Hermes Trismegistus). This is the phrase that is said to hold the key to all of the mysteries. It simply means that which is above is the same as that which is below. The microcosm is yourself. The macrocosm is the Universe. Taken together, the microcosm is the macrocosm, and vice versa. Within each, lies the other; hence, it is through the understanding of one part of this equation (usually the microcosm) that you can actually begin to understand the other.

Truly, science and mysticism are more closely related than we can even begin to imagine.

Knowledge always grows exponentially. The more we know, the greater our ability to learn.

The greater our ability to learn, the faster we are able to expand our knowledge base.

Know thyself were the very words as stated by Pythagoras.

The physical body is a temple of God/dess. We must begin to rebuild the temple of our mind (consciousness).

Science continues to show us that our minds can generate energy that is capable of transforming physical matter.

We already know, for instance, that particles react to our thoughts. Assuredly, this means that we have the power to change the world through our thoughts.

There is a *mental energy* that pervades everything. Could this, then, be the *very image* in which we were created? So, too, then, is God/dess thought.

Could it be that it was our minds (consciousness) that were created in the image of God/dess and not our physical bodies?

Remember, we, too, are creators. I create as I speak, likewise for yourself.

If thoughts affect the world, we must be very careful about what we think and how we think. Sometimes it is far easier to create a destructive thought than an empowering one.

Now is the time to for us to begin *designing our own reality* versus *reacting to what appears to be* the accepted reality.

All have the power to change physical matter with their mind, manifesting, quite literally, all that they desire.

The power of focused conviction and intention are noteworthy components in the overall equation.

Well-directed thought is learned. To manifest one's intention requires [1] sharp, attuned, laser like focus, [2] full sensory visualizations (which I am now able to maintain through Mind Movies, as per page 53) and [3] a profound belief in one's intention.

Any amount of doubt will immediately cancel out the original intention, merely creating more of what you do not want.

The idea of a universal consciousness is indeed possible.

If we can harness the inherent power of prayer groups and healing circles, we have the potential to completely transform our world. This is the *underlying discovery* related to the field of Noetic Science.

The Mayans were avid stargazers, "renowned for their architectural, artistic, mathematical and scientific achievements," [25] leaving us with a series of "super-human sized stone monuments and pyramids with precise calendrical computations." [26]

They had extensive knowledge about astrology, developing calendars based on logic, science and nature, knowing that time was of a qualitative essence. It was not until the advent of the Gregorian Calendar that we began to see time as something outside of ourselves.

This is why we are so hung up on time, especially in the 21st century. It is in seeing time as "something linear, containable, and separate from the organic flowing process of life" [27] that we have created so much unnecessary limitation.

---

[25] 13 Moons of Peace. (2005) *The Mayan Prophecy of 2012* accessed on May 7, 2010 at http://www.13moon.com/prophecy%20page.htm
[26] Ibid.
[27] Ibid.

In keeping with our spiritual natures, we have forgotten that *we*, ourselves, *are time* for "the synchronic order of natural time governs the unfolding of our lives. Time's cycles are found within our bodies and within Nature's daily rhythms cyclic seasons. We have forgotten this, thinking that time is money or that time is the clock, or the relentless progression of work weeks and weekends." [28]

What we have also failed to remember is that "time is the ever-changing, unfolding Now as it synchronistically coordinates the whole living universe" [29] of which we are an integral part.

It must also be remembered that the "Native American traditions, including those of the Lakota, Cherokee and Hopi indicate that *this time in history* is the time of their prophecies, the close of a grand cycle leading to the birth of a new world ... a sixth world of consciousness." [30]

---

[28] 13 Moons of Peace. (2005) *The Mayan Prophecy of 2012* accessed on May 7, 2010 at http://www.13moon.com/prophecy%20page.htm
[29] Ibid.
[30] Braden, Gregg. (1997) *Awakening to Zero Point: The Collective Initiation* (p 4). Bellevue, WA: Radio Bookstore Press.

The Mayan culture was a truly amazing one. Their calendar, an ancient system of time keeping, was predicted to find completion in the year 2012 AD, which is our time; hence, the prophecies of the ancient peoples. This system of time keeping dates back to 18,000 years ago. It is most astounding that their calendar was able to predict our time in history as being the one deemed the lifetime for change.

Such is the purpose of this grand shift for all life forms, including Mother Earth herself. In order to begin to express life through a much higher frequency, a Christed energy if you will, there must be healing and balance. That having been said, "each individual now living upon the Earth is an integral part of The Shift process, playing a vital role of midwife in the birth of a new era of human perception and awareness." [31]

As many well know, the Earth is surrounded by its own magnetic field. It takes approximately 2,000 years for "the fields of magnetics to make one complete rotation around the surface of the Earth." [32]

---

[31] Braden, Gregg. (1997) *Awakening to Zero Point: The Collective Initiation* (p 12). Bellevue, WA: Radio Bookstore Press.
[32] Ibid, p 21.

Over the course of this time span, the intensity of the Earth's magnetic fields have been dropping, more noticeably within our time.

"As magnetics are a function of planetary rotation, a lessening in the intensity of magnetics would seem to indicate a lessening in the rate of the Earth's rotation" [33] as well.

It appears that "the effects of global magnetics are not confined to individuals on a personal level. Variable planetary magnetics provide zones of experience where mass units of consciousness are drawn to feel or work out some form of common experience. When an individual or group consciousness feels that an area no longer feels appropriate, or resonates with them, they are describing their body's sensors to those zones of magnetic density." [34]

The understanding of the nature of these fields becomes "a vital key to understanding mass migrations of large populations, human and animal alike, as well as the unexplained settling of ancient cultures in what may appear

---

[33] Braden, Gregg. (1997) *Awakening to Zero Point: The Collective Initiation* (p 19). Bellevue, WA: Radio Bookstore Press.
[34] Ibid, pp 19-20.

to be very unlikely locations for commerce or spiritual pursuits." [35]

I can remember having watched a documentary on the History channel about Chaco Canyon in northwestern New Mexico. These *zones of magnetic density* clearly had a role to play with regards to this very civilization. What needs to be remembered is that these *lower values of magnetics* are what *provide the opportunity for change*.

This, of course, means that the *exact opposite is true* in areas of *higher magnetics*, whereby stagnation might be perceived. Stagnation, in this sense, merely refers to the fact that one stops progressing, that one stops advancing. Certain individuals would feel these energies as sluggish and dull.

All in all, "these zones simply offer the opportunity for change. How the opportunity is expressed becomes the choice of those experiencing the change." [36]

We are poised on the threshold of a new paradigm of experience, one that is also due to planetary magnetics.

---

[35] Braden, Gregg. (1997) *Awakening to Zero Point: The Collective Initiation* (p 20). Bellevue, WA: Radio Bookstore Press.
[36] Ibid.

It needs to be remembered that the human form is both electrical as well as magnetic. At a time when planetary magnetics were relatively high, this ensured "that to manifest something in this world, we had to be very clear and really choose or desire that which was being envisioned." [37]

The planet, in our time, with considerably lessened magnetics, means that we are now heading in a different direction.

The magnetic fields of the Earth have been dropping over the course of these last 2,000 years. As a result, these lower magnetic fields are *providing the very opportunity for change that we have been wanting*, that we have been praying for.

Not only that, but these lower magnetic fields mean that we are *more rapidly able to manifest what we want* in our lives, because it is in the thinking, feeling and expanding of emotion that we are our own creators.

Indeed, it is in "the space of resonance, attained simply from your patterns of *thought coupled with feeling*, that you may

---

[37] Braden, Gregg. (1997) *Awakening to Zero Point: The Collective Initiation* (p 20). Bellevue, WA: Radio Bookstore Press.

direct energy most efficiently, consciously and with intent. It is in this space that you become the creator of your experiences and may impact the events of your world while regulating the response of your body to that world." [38] This is why it has become so important to carefully monitor your thoughts.

This, then, is where *one must become that which one desires most* in their life. One must become the very experience they most desire for themselves and others: things like love, peace, forgiveness, nonjudgment and compassion.

If we may revert back to the Mayans for a brief moment, it was their belief that the sixth world was actually blank, meaning, of course, that it is up to us, as co-creators, as a human family, to begin creating this new world, this new civilization.

The time to begin is now. Clearly, this is an important time for us to work through issues, both individually as well as collectively.

The Hopi and the Mayan elders did not prophesy that everything would come to an end.

---

[38] Braden, Gregg. (1997) *Awakening to Zero Point: The Collective Initiation* (p 27). Bellevue, WA: Radio Bookstore Press.

They did, however, prophesy that this would be *a time of transition* from one world age to another, thereby entering into a different paradigm.

The word paradigm refers to a conceptual framework, a belief system, an overall perspective, through which we see and interpret the world.

As such, one's paradigm determines what they are able to see, how they think and what they do.

How one views the world, by way of a spiritual traditional, is part of the individual paradigm to which they adhere.

That having been said, paradigms are relative, subjective and personal. We assume that the way in which we see things is actually the way they really are.

Our paradigms, then, become more perceptible to us only when we encounter one that differs from our own.

There are many important questions that one must ask of themselves in order to better understand the paradigm that they follow.

Do I see the world as ......

- *a battlefield*, with good forces being set against evil, all in keeping with an ancient tradition, one that takes us back to the Zoroastrians, the Manichaeans and the Cathars?

- *a classroom* where I come to learn and am put through a multitude of tests?

- *a trap*, one whereby I attempt to disentangle myself in order to ascend to a higher plane of spirituality, of peace, of tranquility?

- *a collection of inanimate objects*, merely to accumulate, thereby stroking my ego?

- *a partner* whereby I attempt to commune more with nature, all in an effort to become more fully human?

- *self*, an interconnected whole with each playing an important role in the overall script of life?

It is in the answering of the questions that follow that you will also become able to better understand your personal paradigms.

What set of structures, or belief system(s), do I operate from?

How are these paradigms serving me in this life?

One way to know yourself, or at least to know where you are now, is to get to know the intricacies of your operating system.

What do I value? What are my needs? What are my feelings? What matters to me? How do I fit into this grand schema called life? How do I know what I know? What is truth?

These are very heady questions.

The more you know about who you are, the easier it is to respond (as opposed to react) to life. Everything we say and do is the expression of a belief about the world. Finding your underlying beliefs will both lead to insights as well as an in-depth understanding.

As one would expect, paradigms shift when we change from one way of thinking to another way of thinking. This can be compared to a revolution, a transformation, a sort of metamorphosis, if you will.

However, this is not something that happens out of the blue and on its own; rather, it is driven by agents of change (which is usually quite difficult).

How is it, then, that paradigms change?

World views emerge to solve problems. For an emerging world view to take hold, the majority have to fully understand, aside from pure abstract intellect, that the current way of thinking is no longer adequate, or sufficient, to solve the problems that we are being faced with.

Being passionate about the change that is needed is not enough to change one's paradigm.

Attempting to suppress the voices of those in disagreement will not allow for a paradigm shift.

We are currently being challenged to combine rational and nonrational (faith, intuition, spiritual insight, nature, body-based wisdom) ways of thinking as a means of embracing this new world view that is emerging.

Science has been revealing that the earth's base resonant frequency is increasing. Science has also been revealing that the magnetic fields of the planet are dropping. Such is reflected, for example, in the shifting migratory patterns of animals.

As we live and walk about the surface of this planet, the frequency in the soil is rising. This affects everything on the planet, accounting for changes in people, animals and plants.

Without judgment, now is the best time for the dismantling of ......

- mental, physical and emotional patterns

- conditioning

- belief systems

- attitudes

- institutions

- thought forms

- programming

...... especially with the frequencies of the planet rising at a considerable rate (which means that what we think or desire is becoming actualized).

The same is happening to our physical bodies. If you feel like you are being pulled in two directions, it is because you are. What is happening to Mother Earth is also happening to her children.

This means that old emotional, mental and spiritual baggage is being loosened, making it easier to let go of what is no longer useful.

You will find that your resistance begins to drop. After all, what is the point in resisting if you remember that what you resist continues to persist?

You will begin to wonder why certain people, places and situations were so important to you in the first place.

Undoubtedly, this change will feel quite chaotic at times, given that things are moving quickly.

In connection with the rising vibrational frequency and the lowering of the magnetic values, our physical bodies are also being transmuted. We are reconnecting our minds to the shared universal consciousness. Our bodies are being activated and altered by this change.

We are transforming. We are becoming who we really are. We are reconnecting with our divine selves.

The frequency of the brain is also being raised. Some people refer to this as going into Zero Point where there is no resistance.

In the dropping of resistance, in the dropping of density, we are discovering that the old programs no longer work. This is where we will truly experience the meaning of *Let Go and Let God.*

It is time for the truth to be revealed.

Truth has power.

As the multitude begin to gravitate toward similar ideas, such will bring forth the impending transformation that is needed.

The so-called second coming is actually the coming of humankind back to themselves. We are the ones of whom the ancients spoke.

We are on the verge of a truly great period of illumination; a new renaissance, if you will.

The so-called Apocalypse is *not* the end of the world. However, it shall be the end of the world as we have long known it to be.

Truth resonates within. This is what we are here to remember.

As far as December 21, 2012 is concerned, yes, something big *is* in the works. This is when we shall experience what has been called the Galactic Alignment, all in accordance with the end of an approximated 26,000 year old cycle. Brilliant skywatchers that they were, the Mayans knew this as well.

This rare astronomical alignment of 2012 will be an alignment between three celestial bodies: [1] the earth at the winter solstice, [2] the sun, and [3] the equilateral plane (or mid-line Galactic Equator) of the Milky Way galaxy.

There are those who believe this solar/galactic alignment shall bring about catastrophic events; hence, all of the doom and gloom, death and destruction.

There are those who believe this solar/galactic alignment shall be little more than a cycle, one that has continued to occur since the birth of this planet, every 26,000 years.

There are those who believe this solar/galactic alignment shall bring about a positive spiritual transformation, one leading to the beginning of a new stage in the development of human consciousness, thereby marking a new era in the history of humankind

The Mayans, themselves, understood what the great shift and energy cycles were all about.

Nowhere in the glyphs that are left did they indicate that the earth was coming to an end.

Instead, they spoke of one of the highest vibrations that would return, all coinciding with the Galactic Alignment of December 2012.

The Mayans believed that such would result in *the end of an old time* and *the beginning of a new consciousness* for the planet. In fact, there are a great many who believe that this shift of the ages has already begun.

We are now changing the fabric of what has long been thought impossible and/or unchangeable.

In talking about ascension, there are many interrelated terms being used to describe the same thing: the Shift, the Great Transformation, the return to Christ Consciousness, Awakening, Empowerment, Zero Point, the Golden Age.

Quite simply, ascension means *returning to our natural state of light.* In waking up, we are able to let go of old dogma and perceptions, quickly concluding that love is the answer.

As our individual vibrations rise, so, too, are we raising the vibrations of the planet.

Ascension is a level of consciousness whereby we experience limitless union with the oneness of all life. We are here to become our highest possible selves.

One can best prepare for ascension by [1] meditating with their inner spirit on a daily basis, [2] keeping their attention focused on the light (the greater good) at all times, [3] developing spiritual non-attachment, [4] learning to attune to their higher guidance system, and [5] engaging in regular spiritual activities that serve to refine their energy, thereby raising their vibration.

Like myself, you shall also find that as your vibrational and energetic frequencies increase, you will be open to [1] spiritual expansion (transition), [2] transcendence from polarity (a synergistic effect whereby the compassionate allowance and embracement of duality actually results in one's becoming more than the polarities themselves), and [3] the natural state of transformation (the self-realization and self-actualization of who you really are).

There is "also the idea that when you have attained this extraordinary state called super-consciousness, called enlightenment, that there is nowhere to go; that this is the end and you have attained perfection! It is not so. You are *not to attain perfection* in this transformation; you *already are perfect*. When the transformation comes, you will not be more perfect. You will simply be in the realization of the perfection that you are in this now and in the realization of your own perfection." [39]

---

[39] King, Jani. (2001) *2012, Spirituality, The Mayan Calendar and YOU* blog accessed on May 7, 2010 at http://www.maya12-21-2012.com/blogger.html

Further to this, "nobody will be left behind. Why? Because this transition is about love, and love means no separation. It is about love. It is about your truth. It is the most exciting adventure" [40] that we have been involved with for the last 26,000 years. We have the chance to transcend the old ways and learn to live in peace and harmony with the Cosmos.

Truly, there is *nothing to fear* so please do not allow yourself to be drawn into the unnecessary perceptions of others.

While the planet is changing and the overall consciousness of its inhabitants is clearly on the rise, the world is not about to come to a drastic end.

It is important, however, to know what you can do to navigate these changes, which has been the *intent* of this book.

Meditation is important during this ascension process in that we are better able to remain in the heart, staying centered in the Higher Self. Meditation is what bridges the dimensions that exist.

---

[40] King, Jani. (2001) *2012, Spirituality, The Mayan Calendar and YOU* blog accessed on May 7, 2010 at http://www.maya12-21-2012.com/blogger.html

This reconnecting with Source is what triggers the peace that passes the understanding of the mind. The heart needs to be immersed in true meditation. The entirety of one's day can become a full meditation.

In essence, by 2012, many people will have become enlightened, meaning that they will have embraced openness, honesty, a love for all life, and a belief in the divine cosmic plan for all. This is where we are headed. We are poised at the gateway to a new world of consciousness. Something new is about to be born as we shed the skin of our old, materialistic, selves.

In going through a restructuring of the physical body, do whatever you feel needs to be done to support this process. We are consciously living this ascension process. We must become immersed in oneness, unity and following the heart.

Our bodies are being fine tuned. We are going through this process with each other and with Mother Earth.

We need to stop comparing ourselves to others because people ascend differently. It may not be that everyone that you see *is* ascending. Perhaps they do not need to.

As the planetary frequencies rise higher and higher, our frequencies are also increasing.

We need to remember there is no end. We are never ending. We are eternal. We are one with the Creator.

Everything is connected by energy. We are energy. We live in energy. Energy is constantly flowing through us and around us.

As people learn more about these energies and frequencies, they are able to experience greater amounts of this cosmic energy. Those who are quite adept at meditation often feel a significant increase in their energy because they are tapping into the natural, and universal, flow of energy.

Adept or not, all of us can assist in this overall process of spiritual evolution. How do we do our part?

By thinking about love.

By focusing on the interconnectedness that exists.

By speaking to others with love.

By treating all in a loving manner.

You must *see yourself as one with everyone and everything*.

You must *act like you are one with everyone and everything*.

While the accomplishing specifics shall be different for each person, the outcome shall be the same.

If we live each day with an accepting and compassionate demeanor, choosing to create love in the unique circumstances that are encountered individually, we will begin to make a difference.

We are always attracting energies. Remember, like attracts like. We are always processing the energies that we send out. We are always processing the energies that we receive. We are always transforming and releasing energies via our vibratory signatures. As a result, our energy greatly impacts those around us.

That having been said, we certainly *can* help in the energy transformation of the planet. As little as we want, or as much as we want, such becomes our choice.

There is no greater work than this when it comes to each other. There is no greater work than this when it comes to Mother Gaia.

The Grail: What Might It Be?

It is in the coming together of all duality (male and female, Yin and Yang, day and night, life and death, happiness and sadness, old and new, body and spirit, same and different), and the embracement and acceptance of the dual parts of the self (light and dark), that one begins to understand that nonduality becomes the reality. Ultimately, it is this that shall lead to the healing of all, including the patriarchal institutions of old.

The reading of *A Travel in Time to Grand Pré*, a previous publication of mine, will further serve to enlighten you, the reader, as to what I am endeavoring to say (refer to the chapter entitled *Message for the 21st Century*).

When the two become as one, therein shall you find the true Holy Grail.

What does this mean?

Is it deliberately meant to be cryptic in nature?

Is it meant only for those who have eyes to see and ears to hear?

Every individual is on a journey of self; a journey of rediscovery, if you will.

In the integration of the dualistic parts of the self (light and dark, love and hate, masculine and feminine), we are able to revert back to our truest nature: one of compassion and compassionate allowing; thereby leading to the reestablishment of one's creative powers through the balance of the self.

It shall be in this rediscovering of our true selves that we will have found the Holy Grail. While the Holy Grail is the same for everyone, the process and experience(s) for each individual shall be vastly different; hence, we all become the Grail.

In having identified that there is something great at work, every time you are at peace, so, too, are you enlightened. Inner peace is probably the most important thing that can be attained. When you experience inner peace, you are truly happy and content with your Self. Your state of mind is a quiet mind and you are completely connected to God/dess.

God/dess and peace are synonymous. Inner turmoil is what suffocates your spirit, thereby preventing you from living from your higher self, unable to see life with a greater sense of clarity.

Enlightenment (the Holy Grail) is a state of being whereby you are reunited with your true spiritual self. It is this connectedness, this freedom of the self, that leads us to the ultimate and definitive realization that we are all one, thus imbuing our bodies with a sense of inner peace that allows us to joyfully accept and live life as per our creation.

Was Yeshua ben Yosef (Jesus) of a royal bloodline? It is my belief and understanding that he was.

Did he marry and have children? Most definitely.

Is he the Holy Grail? Absolutely.

Is he showing us the way to the Holy Grail? Uneqivocally.

We must take the time to revisit the message that he attempted to share with us 2,000 years ago, as opposed to that which has been corrupted, hijacked, fabricated and manufactured in his name, for therein lies the necessary truth(s).

Seek ye knowledge and ye shall find the truth that liberates. Seek ye discipline in the persisting with positive thoughts. Seek ye the joy of creating, the joy of learning, the joy of experiencing. Seek ye the realm of infinite possibilities for therein ye shall find the all. Seek ye the seer that ye be.

How can we continue to harm others, in the name of God (under the guise of religion, which was created by man), simply because they are of a different race, a different nationality, a different tribe, a different class, a different sex, a different sexuality, a different religion, a different belief system?

The moment one begins to question these outlandish practices, these separatist practices, these elitist practices, such is indicative of the spiritual path.

"Those who know not that they are one, act not as one. Those who act not as one, create not love, but suffering and disharmony. What you create, you receive." [41]

One's state of consciousness mirrors their state of awareness of the world. This awareness is reflected in the way they view the world, the way they interpret and understand the world, the way they interact with everyone and everything.

---

[41] Peniel, Jon. (1997) *The Children of the Law of One and The Lost Teachings of Atlantis* (p 61). Alamosa, CO: Network.

Essentially, one's state of consciousness is fully reflective of the paradigms, beliefs and programming that they conform to. All is usually in sync with a person's point of view. However, "consciousness is dominant, and if there is a shift to a higher or lower state, the new consciousness can alter and override a person's beliefs and programming in order to match the new level of consciousness." [42]

If everything in the universe is made of the same substance, so, too, are we made of this same substance. Therefore, all is interdependent and connected. Even though we can think we are separate, even though we can believe we are separate, even though we can act like we are separate, in truth, there is no separation. Therein lies the illusion.

It is in the focusing on the illusion of separation that one begins to concentrate solely on themselves. This is where the me, me, me of the ego comes into play. It has been through attention and energy to self, that complete and total selfishness was created.

Good and evil are relative only to the ego. "The ego doesn't want us looking for God because when we find God, the illusion of being an ego will be destroyed. One cannot see

---

[42] Peniel, Jon. (1997) *The Children of the Law of One and The Lost Teachings of Atlantis* (p 65). Alamosa, CO: Network.

God and continue to live as a separate person. Each and every day we will watch the mind carefully and destroy our divisiveness. We will stop separating and start uniting. We will stop hating and start loving." [43]

The sole cure for all of the problems that we are hereby faced with lies in *losing this separate consciousness* and *regaining oneness consciousness*. This can only be attained through acts of unselfish love.

Look to both Jesus and Buddha as important and living examples of compassion, kindness, caring, giving, sharing and harmlessness.

The only person we have the power to change is ourselves. While that may seem miniscule at best, in truth, it becomes monumental.

As we focus on affecting the needed change within, as ripples traverse outward into the majestic realms of the universe, the world comes one step closer to peace. To change the consciousness of the world, the first tenant becomes that of focusing on ourselves.

---

[43] Walker III, Ethan. (2003) *The Mystic Christ: The Light of Non-Duality and the Path of Love According to the Life and Teachings of Jesus* (p 49). Norman, OK: Devi Press Inc.

Changes takes place, one person at a time.

There are many things that clutter us up on a spiritual level.

- nagging anxieties

- jealousy

- anger

- resentment

- regret

- fear

- guilt

- skepticism

- cynicism

- failure to be true to one's self

- greed

- constant busyness

- negativity

These are the issues that weigh us down with a heavy heart. These are the issues that leave us feeling depressed, powerless, unbalanced. These are the issues that hinder our spiritual growth.

It is imperative that you find a place of solitude, away from work, away from the television, away from cell phones and emails. In the silence, take the time to pay attention to what your inner (and intuitive) teacher has to say. Silence and stillness are healthy for the soul.

Meditation, a union of mind and body, is an adventure of self-discovery.

Scientists are now discovering that meditation has a biological effect on the body. It has even been suggested, by means of a small scale study, that meditation can boost parts of the brain as well as the immune system.

Meditation can be used to expand the paradigm to which you adhere. Meditation leads to peace, tranquility and equanimity of mind. In keeping, equanimity of mind leads to self-realization and/or the super-conscious state of mind.

Kindness, goodness, compassion, caring, giving, unselfish love and harmlessness ... such is *the way*. These are the earmarks of true spirituality.

Any individual who wants to grow, who wants to attain spiritual enlightenment, who wants to be a really good person, must first and foremost completely reevaluate their beliefs.

They must be willing to ask themselves why they adhere to such beliefs. They must be willing to ask themselves where they came from. They must be willing to ask themselves if they are willing to embrace change in order to welcome spiritual growth.

Who you are, and what you do with universal consciousness, is key. This is why, when you have realized (achieved) universal consciousness, it is called enlightenment or illumination. It is as if a light switch has been turned on in a life that was, up until that point, lived in darkness.

Universal consciousness is attained when a person has a lasting experience in which they see through the illusion of separateness, thereby losing their separate consciousness. It is then that their consciousness merges with the universe; thus they experience being one with the universe.

The illusion of separateness has no choice but to dissolve in the awareness of oneness. As a result, the separate self (ego) seems to die and a rebirth occurs.

One's consciousness is transcended and transformed.

When universal consciousness is properly experienced, the individual is never the same. From that moment on, all things are understood in the light of the universal picture. Selfishness has become a thing of the past.

The closer one gets to attaining universal consciousness, the greater their point of view becomes.

We are not the body. We are spirit.

We are the I AM, created from the very breath and thought of the Creator. We, too, are creators.

Know your true self and you will know the true story.

Know your whole self and you will know the wholeness of the truth.

Awakening is simply abiding in one's natural state. We are pure existence. Although thoughts may happen due to the fact that the brain's automatic patterns may happen, just like the sun rises and sets, we are *not* our thoughts. This, too, is key.

Each is complete. Each is one. Each is perfect. Each is a divine masterpiece.

It is only through the death experience than one can fully understand that which is life. This does not have to be a literal death; rather, it can be a symbolic death, as in the death of the egoic mind.

Honor, integrity and service to all life are also key.

If one but takes the time to look about them with *spiritual eyes*, one will find beauty and harmony in abundance. There are individuals who do not yet understand that an increase in one's vibratory level serves to bring about remarkable changes.

The more enlightened we become, the less likely we are attracted to the darker energies that exist, gradually pulling away from their influence. In so doing, we reclaim our power, an absolute necessity, for we, alone, have been responsible for allowing others to impose restrictions upon us.

We are vibrational beings. That which we focus upon, with emotion and intent, becomes our reality.

Dharma means carrier of goodness and wholesomeness. Hu means light, as in you are the light of God. When you spread darkness, you go opposite your dharma. When you slander someone, you go opposite your dharma.

We are carriers of goodness and wholesomeness. We are carriers of light.

There exists an inherent difference between the ancient mysteries and the *Bible*.

Why is it that the mysteries are all about the God that exists within (meaning man as God) whereas the *Bible* became the God outside of you and above you?

Therein lies the *illusion of separation* that was *deliberately created* for a multitude of reasons, the chief ones being power, control and greed. Religion was established as the official toll bridge to heaven; one that continues to request, and/or dictate, death and destruction as its sole fee.

You are God yourself, said Buddha.

The Kingdom of God exists within, said Yeshua ben Yosef (Jesus).

These works that I do, you, too, can do ... and greater, said Yeshua ben Yosef (Jesus).

In our search for God/dess, could it be that we have, in truth, been searching for ourselves?

Could it be that the only difference between God/dess and ourselves is that we have forgotten that we are divine?

Just as God in *Genesis* is described as being more than one, so, too, is God/dess found in the many.

It is true spirituality that recognizes the *dominion of peace*. In keeping, "spiritual people remain non-involved in world affairs and, even when the world seeks to pull them into its theatrical, glamorized arena, they remain non-attached and peaceful." [44] With no need to change the world, they "see the simple beauty and perfection of all that exists and feel a compassion for all life rather than an emotional involvement." [45]

As this rekindled awareness grows exponentially upon this planet, it shall serve to uplift others, with results being noted as remarkable increases in the mass consciousness of humankind.

Clearly, this is a time to rejoice.

---

[44] Self and Spirit: Spirituality, Enlightenment & Higher Consciousness website. Article *What Are The Characteristics Of A True Spiritual Person?* retrieved on July 2, 2010 at http://illumen8.com/what-are-the-characteristics-of-a-true-spiritual-person.html
[45] Ibid.

Too often we live our lives with limiting beliefs. It is imperative that we come to realize, accept and acknowledge that we are limitless beings.

How best can we rid ourselves of programmed beliefs? How best can we rid ourselves of limiting beliefs?

Some choose to work with affirmations (which only work as long as you *believe* and *feel* what you are saying). It is much too easy to sabotage affirmations if what you are saying and feeling is not in alignment with each other.

Some may attempt guided meditation. Others create vision boards. Speaking for myself, I was relieved to discover Mind Movies, an absolutely phenomenal metaphysical tool (refer back to page 53).

If we are not successful in neutralizing these limiting beliefs, we are not in a position to open up to allowing the Universe to bring forth that which we really want.

It is important to remember that *all we experience has been, and continues to be, attracted by us*, depending on our thoughts, feelings, emotions and intent.

153

According to quantum physics, the physical world is created by its observer (namely, us). This energy, then, becomes structured into the matter that we see in the physical world, depending on our own individual expectations. The world around us is reflected in what we believe.

It is absolutely imperative that you completely eliminate several powerful words from your vocabulary – NO, NOT, DON'T, CAN'T, SHOULDN'T, COULDN'T – because the *use of these words merely serves to attract more of what you do not want* into your life.

Our thoughts create our feelings. Our feelings create our vibrations.

In every moment of every day, we are sending out vibrations. They can be easily identified as negative or positive, by the feeling(s) being experienced.

One can learn to reset their vibrations from negative to positive just by choosing different words and different thoughts.

Emotional Freedom Techniques (EFT) is a very powerful tool that can be used to *neutralize* fears and blockages.

The process in keeping with EFT is one that requires tapping certain energy points (meridians) of the body while focusing on an issue that needs to be resolved.

Emotional wellness is key.

Emotional wellness is easily identified when you are able to feel a sense of overall comfort and acceptance with the full range of emotions and feelings that one can experience.

As we strive to meet our emotional needs in a constructive way, we are better able to maintain good mental health, a positive attitude and a strong sense of self.

EFT [46] provides a bridge between two well known healing modalities: meridian based therapies and mind body therapies, blending both disciplines into one procedure.

The cause of all negative emotions is a disruption in the energy system of the body. As has been identified in a previous chapter, our bodies are electrical in nature.

Over 5,000 years ago, it was the Chinese who discovered a subtle energy in the body, one that could not be seen, felt or identified with the senses.

---

[46] World Center for EFT (Emotional Freedom Techniques) located at http://www.eftuniverse.com/

Energy disturbances can be located in the physical body *before* actually manifesting into abnormal patterns, thereby disrupting healthy cellular organization and growth.

These meridians are the pathways, or energy highways, through which both positive and negative energy circulates throughout the body. Connected with every organ in the body, the diminishing of one's chi, or life force, leads to poor organ functioning, discomfort and ill health.

Balancing this energy is crucial to living a healthy and peaceful life. EFT tapping serves to help balance and restore energy blockages connected to the meridian system.

Ho'oponopono is the ancient Hawaiian self-help method that clears the body of toxic energies, thereby allowing for the presence of divine thoughts, words, deeds and actions. It means to *make right*. According to those who avail of this method, errors are created from thoughts that are associated with painful memories from the past.

In essence, Ho'oponopono offers a way, through love, gratitude and forgiveness, to clear the energy of painful thoughts (errors) which cause imbalance and disease.

Dr. Ihaleakala Hew Len healed an entire hospital of mentally ill people using this technique. According to Dr. Len, we can either live from memory or from inspiration.

Memories are merely old programs that keep replaying themselves, over and over and over again.

When we are fully present in our zero state, this is a state whereby we have zero limits: no memories, no thoughts, no identity; only the divine exists.

All problems begin as thoughts. When you employ Ho'oponopono, the divinity residing within neutralizes and/or purifies these painful thoughts. These thoughts can be related to people, places, events and situations.

In using Ho'oponopono, there are four phrases that you repeat out loud to yourself.

I love you (meaning that you are allowing yourself to be open to all of the love that is coming to you).

I am sorry (meaning that you are apologizing to the divinity within for your erroneous program (thoughts) even without knowing the cause).

Please forgive me (meaning that you are asking the divinity within for forgiveness).

Thank you (meaning that you are expressing gratitude for the opportunity that clearing an erroneous program gives to you).

As you repeat these four phrases, you must focus your intent on addressing the divinity within.

As we heal ourselves, we participate in the healing of the world around us. <u>Zero Limits</u> by Joe Vitale is a wonderful book about Ho'oponopono.

There are also additional energetic methods that can be used to clear the meridians of energy blockages.

<u>Reiki</u> is a Japanese technique for stress reduction and relaxation that also promotes healing. Administered by the laying on of hands, it is based on the idea that an unseen life force energy (understood by the Chinese over 5,000 years ago) flows through us.

The practitioner uses his or her hands in the energy field of the client to facilitate healing. The client remains fully clothed and in a laying position. The practitioner usually moves his or her hands at a distance of a few inches from the body, although touching can be involved.

If one's life force energy, or chi, is low, we are more likely to get sick or feel stress. If one's life force energy, or chi, is high, we are more capable of being happy and healthy.

To learn more, visit <u>The International Center for Reiki Training</u>. [47]

<u>Crystal Therapy</u> involves the use of crystals to attempt healing by affecting personal, and environmental, vibration as a means to facilitating balance and healing.

Gems, stones and crystals are generally laid on the body over the chakra points. As each chakra resonates to a particular color, laying a stone of that color over the chakra allows the chakras to open, align and blend with each other, thereby facilitating balance. When the chakra system is balanced, the physical body is able to experience healing.

It has been said that Crystal Therapy is an ancient art, originating, as some believe, in ancient Egypt. Others believe the form to be even older, possibly dating back to both Lemuria and Atlantis.

While I resonate with a great many different stone types, some of my favorite stones are those containing Lithium, such as Golden C, Lepidolite, Kunzite, Hiddenite and Lithium Quartz, in that they serve to assist me in the calming of my anxieties when I am unable to meditate.

---

[47] http://www.reiki.org/

In keeping with the lore and metaphysical properties attributed to gems, stones and crystals, while unsubstantiated from a scientific perspective, each individual must assume responsibility for their use of, and/or misuse of, this information.

Chios Energy Healing, although relatively new, is a very comprehensive energy healing system that employs powerful and effective aura and chakra healing techniques, nearly all of which are unique to Chios.

To learn more, visit the Chios Energy Healing [48] website of founder Stephen H. Barrett.

Therapeutic Touch is an effective healing modality widely used and accepted in clinical practice. It is a modern application of several ancient healing practices which use the laying on of hands.

The practitioner uses his or her hands in the energy field of the client to facilitate healing. The client remains fully clothed and in a laying position. The practitioner usually moves his or her hands at a distance of a few inches from the body, although touching can be involved.

---

[48] http://www.chioshealing.com/

Therapeutic Touch is based on the concept that humans are complex energy fields.

It is the goal of Therapeutic Touch to rebalance the flow of energy as a support to the healing process.

Healing Touch is a biofield therapy that is an energy based approach to health and healing.

This approach uses touch to influence the human energy system, specifically the energy field that surrounds the body, as well as the energy centers (chakras) that control the energy flow from the energy field to the physical body.

The goal in Healing Touch is to restore harmony and balance to the human energy system. It is most helpful in promoting relaxation, reducing pain and managing stress.

Quantum Touch is a method of natural healing that works with the life force energy of the body to promote optimal wellness.

Life force energy, also known as chi (Chinese) or prana (Sanskrit), is the flow of energy that sustains all life. Quantum Touch teaches one how to focus, amplify and direct this energy.

All healing is self-healing. The body has an extraordinary intelligence and ability to heal itself. Given the right energetic, emotional, nutritional and spiritual environments, the natural state of the body is that of perfect health.

Although all healing is, indeed, self-healing, Quantum Touch, by combining various breathing and body awareness exercises, can help other people heal with their own healing process.

To learn more, visit the <u>Quantum Touch</u> [49] website.

---

[49] http://www.quantumtouch.com/

Excerpted segments from my novel, *A Travel in Time to Grand Pré*, are being introduced here. Yeshua ben Yosef, the eldest son born to Yosef and Miryam, is the author.

I am one of you, meaning that I, too, am of the brotherhood of man. All have come here to experience and understand the conclusiveness of God in this physical form.

If you but take the time to see, to feel, to reflect, to meditate within, you will see that God exists everywhere, within all things and within all beings.

We are a melding of *God-man* (the mind of God expressing in human form) and *man-God* (physical man expressing the God within), a combined merger of spiritual and physical that serves to continue the expansion of the Father into forever.

In this light, you need not seek anything outside of your Being, for all that you need resides within.

As you come into your own alignment with truth, you, too, will see that anything that does not serve you, anything that is not in resonance, shall fall away.

You shall also be able to attest that it is in this release and letting go, something better *always* comes along.

The only constant in life is change.

Be not afraid of change.

Change allows all to Be (as they are) and to Become (who they truly are).

Many have forgotten their divinity.

In so doing, they believe themselves to be separate from God. Within this forgetting lies limited beliefs, opinions and judgments, none of which are functional in navigating your way through to the higher expression of the God within.

There is a way to remembering the sacredness of all life, and that is the way of nonjudgment.

As you become aware of your limiting beliefs, you better understand that your interactions with others are driven by *what you believe to be true* about the person.

Sadly, these limiting beliefs *never* reflect the actual truth, a truth that states all is one.

As you gain in universal awareness, you quickly come to the realization that your divinity is also theirs as well.

When you respond to people with love and compassion, you readily move from conflict to harmony. Such is the very freedom sought by all.

When you remember, embrace and share your divinity, you free others to walk their truth. You become accepting of their truth, for such is whom they are.

Living a life of gratitude, trust, love and peace is what generates more of the same, thereby continuously affecting those around you in a positive way.

Radiating the complete and total realization of being one with the Creator is what enables, and allows, others to feel safe and secure within your very presence.

For many of your brothers and sisters, this is *exactly* what may be needed to begin to elicit an arresting change within their very Being.

It is impossible not to experience the effects of such love and acceptance.

It is known that thought must first exist before manifestation of thought, also known as creation, can take place. In that alignment, we have the ability to manifest whatever we wish, all for the sole purpose of enhancing the life wisdom that we continue to accrue, life after life after life.

We create our lives through our own thought processes. Everything you think, you will feel. Everything you feel, you will manifest. Everything you manifest serves to create the condition(s) of your life.

Every word we utter expresses some feeling within our souls. Every word we utter serves to create the conditions of our lives. This is a direct fusion of thought with emotion.

Many will have heard the phrase *like attracts like*, which means that what one gives thought to attracts, unto itself, the very same.

In the end, it is still a matter of choice and free will.

Thought is the true giver of life that never dies, that can never be destroyed. All have used it to think themselves into life, for thought is your link to the mind of God.

We *get* what we speak. We *are* what we think. We *become* what we direct our energies to. We *become* that which we conclude ourselves to be.

If any of these words have resonated with you, I suggest that you purchase a copy of *A Travel in Time to Grand Pré* so that you may read Yeshua's message in its entirety.

The unlocking of our minds must continue.

Mental restructuring is the key to opening the door.

Yeshua

Commissioned by Nick Bunick

Reprinted with permission.

Love Is The New Religion

On the surface of our world right now

There is war, violence, and craziness

And things may seem dark.

But calmly and quietly

At the same time

Something is happening underground.

An inner revolution is taking place

And certain individuals

Are being called to a higher light.

It is a silent revolution

From the inside out

From the ground up.

Veracity At Its Best

This is a global co-operation

That has sleeper cells in every nation

It is a planetary Spiritual Conspiracy.

You won't likely see us on TV.

You won't read about us in the newspaper.

You won't hear from us on the radio.

We are in every country and culture of the world.

In cities big and small, mountains and valleys,

In farms and villages, tribes and remote islands.

Most of us work anonymously

Seeking not recognition of name

But profound transformation of life.

Working quietly behind the scenes

You could pass by one of us on the street

And not even notice.

Veracity At Its Best

We go undercover

Not concerned for who takes the final credit

But simply that the work gets done.

Many of us may seem to have normal jobs,

But behind the external storefront

Is where the deeper work takes place.

With the individual and collective power

Of our minds and hearts

We spread passion, knowledge, and joy to all.

Some call us the Conscious Army

As together

We co-create a new world.

Our orders come from the Spiritual Intelligence Agency

Instructing us to drop soft, secret love bombs

When no one is looking.

Veracity At Its Best

Poems ~ Hugs ~ Music

Photography ~ Smiles ~ Kind words

Movies ~ Meditation and prayer ~ Dance ~ Websites

Social activism ~ Blogs ~ Random acts of kindness ......

We each express ourselves

In our own unique ways

With our own unique gifts and talents.

Be the change you want to see in the world

Is the motto that fills our hearts.

We know this is the path to profound transformation.

We know that quietly and humbly

Individually and collectively

We have the power of all the oceans combined.

Veracity At Its Best

At first glance our work is not even visible.

It is slow and meticulous

Like the formation of mountains.

And yet with our combined efforts

Entire tectonic plates

Are being shaped and moved for centuries to come.

Love is the religion we come to share

And you don't need to be highly educated

Or have exceptional knowledge to understand it.

Love arises from the intelligence of the heart

Embedded in the timeless evolutionary pulse

Of all living things.

Be the change you want to see in the world.

No one else can do it for you.

Yet don't forget, we are all here supporting you.

We are now recruiting.

Perhaps you will join us

Or already have.

For in this spiritual conspiracy

All are welcome, and all are loved.

The door is always open.

Written by Brian Piergrossi and excerpted from *The Big Glow: Insight, Inspiration, Peace and Passion.*

While you can visit Brian's website [50] for additional information, please also take the time to watch the Spiritual Conspiracy video [51] on YouTube, set to music and containing the very lyrics shared herein.

---

[50] http://TheBigGlow.com

[51] http://www.youtube.com/watch?v=mM7KddDERd0

The End

What is an ending of a book, if not a new and unforeseen beginning?

As written by Gary Crowley in *From Here to Here: Turning Toward Enlightenment* … "Awakening to enlightenment is a journey from here to here, not from here to there. There is nowhere to go and nothing to be attained. Enlightenment is simply an awakening to what has *always* been the case." [52]

We are *not* isolated beings living desperate lives. We have far more power that we realize. As individuals, each has the ability to improve their lives. We simply cannot live lives of marginal existence any longer.

I wish for you much joy in the journey, as you also make your way to the peaceable kingdom of wholeness and completeness, one that already exists within. It is not the destination that is necessarily of the greatest importance, but the very discoveries you make along the way; a journey of giving, oneness and destiny.

---

[52] Crowley, Gary. (2006) *From Here to Here*: *Turning Toward Enlightenment* (p 3). Boulder, CO: GL Design.

Addendum

My thanks to William H. Marshall, author of *Power Affirmations: Power Positive Conditioning For Your Subconscious Mind*, for having inspired me with his words; words that so resonated with me that I have to share here, but with my own adaptation.

I see part of my mission as making a measureable positive difference on our world. The quality of our world depends upon the quality of our thoughts as individuals.

If the majority of individuals are positive and successful, then society itself will naturally be positive, successful and prosperous.

If, however, the majority of people are negative, hateful and unsuccessful, then people will live in unhappy, unsuccessful, perhaps even dire circumstances.

In keeping with the phenomenal text *As A Man Thinketh* by James Allen ... so, too, thinketh's a society.

Looking at it this way, each of us has an individual responsibility to be positive and to help others be positive. If you, too, will take it upon yourself to condition your mind to be positive, to help other people, to be successful, to fill your life with happiness, then I have accomplished one of my primary objectives.

Likewise, if you are able to share information about my books with others, and the information contained within is of some benefit to them, as well as to yourself, then my purpose is fulfilled.

For you see, if *you* help two people, and *they* help two people, and so on and so forth, it is through the miraculous power of compounded growth that *we* can create massive social improvement for all.

Bibliography

Ambrose, Kala. (2007) *9 Life Altering Lessons: Secrets of the Mystery Schools Unveiled.*

Austin, June. (2006) *Genesis of Man.*

Braden, Gregg. (1995) *Awakening to Zero Point: The Collective Initiation.*

Braden, Gregg. (1997) *Walking Between the Worlds: The Science of Compassion.*

Braden, Gregg. (2000) *The Isaiah Effect: Decoding the Lost Science of Prayer and Prophecy.*

Braden, Gregg. (2000) *Beyond Zero Point: The Journey to Compassion.*

Braden, Gregg. (2004) *The God Code: The Secret of Our Past, The Promise of Our Future.*

Braden, Gregg. (2004) *The Divine Name: Sounds of the God Code.* (Audio Book)

Braden, Gregg. (2005) *The Lost Mode of Prayer.* (Audio CD)

Braden, Gregg. (2005) *Unleashing The Power of The God Code: The Mystery and Meaning of the Message in Our Cells*. (Audio CD)

Braden, Gregg. (2005) *An Ancient Magical Prayer: Insights from the Dead Sea Scrolls*. (Audio Book)

Braden, Gregg. (2005) *Speaking the Lost Language of God: Awakening the Forgotten Wisdom of Prayer, Prophecy and the Dead Sea Scrolls*. (Audio Book)

Braden, Gregg. (2005) *Awakening the Power of A Modern God: Unlock the Mystery and Healing of Your Spiritual DNA*. (Audio Book)

Braden, Gregg. (2006) *Secrets of The Lost Mode of Prayer*.

Braden, Gregg. (2007) *The Divine Matrix: Bridging Time, Space, Miracles and Belief*.

Breathnach, Sarah Ban. (1996) *Simple Abundance: A Daybook of Comfort and Joy*.

Breathnach, Sarah Ban. (2000) *The Simple Abundance Companion: Following Your Authentic Path To Something More*.

Bunick, Nick. (1998) *In God's Truth*.

Bunick, Nick. (2010) *Time for Truth: A New Beginning.*

Chopra, Deepak. (1998) *The Path to Love: Spiritual Strategies for Healing.*

Chopra, Deepak. (2005) *Peace Is The Way: Bringing War and Violence to An End.*

Coelho, Paulo. (1998) *The Alchemist.*

Coelho, Paulo. (2003) *Warrior Of The Light.*

Das, Lama Surys. (1998) *Awakening the Buddha Within.*

Das, Lama Surys. (2000) *Awakening to the Sacred: Creating a Spiritual Life From Scratch.*

Das, Lama Surys. (2001) *Awakening the Buddhist Heart: Integrating Love, Meaning and Connection into Every Part of Your Life.*

Das, Lama Surys. (2003) *Living Kindness: The Buddha's Ten Guiding Principles for a Blessed Life.*

Das, Lama Surys. (2003) *Letting Go of the Person You Used To Be: Lessons on Change, Loss and Spiritual Transformation.*

Doucette, Michele. (2010) *A Travel in Time to Grand Pré.* (second edition)

Doucette, Michele. (2010) *The Ultimate Enlightenment For 2012: All We Need Is Ourselves.*

Doucette, Michele. (2010) *Turn Off The TV: Turn On Your Mind.*

Dyer, Wayne. (1993) *Manifest Your Destiny: The Nine Spiritual Principles For Getting Everything That You Want.*

Dyer, Wayne. (2002) *Getting in the Gap: Making Conscious Contact with God Through Meditation.* (Book and CD)

Gawain, Shakti. (1993) *Living In The Light: A Guide to Personal and Planetary Transformation.*

Gawain, Shakti. (1999) *The Four Levels of Healing.*

Gawain, Shakti. (2000) *The Path of Transformation: How Healing Ourselves Can Change The World.*

Gawain, Shakti. (2003) *Reflections in The Light: Daily Thoughts and Affirmations.*

Gelb, Michael. (2005) *Da Vinci Decoded.*

Hansard, Christopher. (2003) *The Tibetan Art of Positive Thinking.*

Hicks, Esther and Hicks, Jerry. (2004) *Ask and It Is Given: Learning to Manifest Your Desires.*

Hicks, Esther and Hicks, Jerry. (2004) *The Teachings of Abraham: Well-Being Cards.*

Hicks, Esther and Hicks, Jerry. (2005) *The Amazing Power of Deliberate Intent: Living the Art of Allowing.*

Hicks, Esther and Hicks, Jerry. (2006) *The Law of Attraction: The Basics of the Teachings of Abraham.*

Hicks, Esther and Hicks, Jerry. (2008) *The Astonishing Power of Emotions: Let Your Feelings Be Your Guide.*

Hicks, Esther and Hicks, Jerry. (2009) *The Vortex: Where The Law of Attraction Assembles all Cooperative Relationships.*

Icke, David. (2005) *Infinite Love is the Only Truth: Everything Else is Illusion.*

Ingram, Julia. (2004) *The Lost Sisterhood: The Return of Mary Magdalene, the Mother Mary, and Other Holy Women.*

Johnson, Bettye. (2005) *Secrets of the Magdalene Scrolls: The Forbidden Truth of the Life and Times of Mary Magdalene.*

Johnson, Bettye. (2007) *Mary Magdalene, Her Legacy.*

Johnson, Bettye. (2008) *Awakening the Genie Within.*

Koven, Jean-Claude. (2004) *Going Deeper: How To Make Sense of Your Life When Your Life Makes No Sense.*

Kribbe, Pamela. (2008) *The Jeshua Channelings: Christ Consciousness in a New Era.*

Lama, Dalai. (2004) *The Wisdom of Forgiveness: Intimate Conversations and Journey.*

Lyons, Lona. (2007) *The Magdalene Dispensation.*

Lyons, Lona. (2008) *Daughter of Magdalene.*

McTaggart, Lynne. (2003) *The Field: The Quest For The Secret Force Of The Universe.*

McTaggart, Lynne. (2008) *The Intention Experiment: Using Your Thoughts to Change Your Life and the World.*

Millman, Dan. (2000) *Way of the Peaceful Warrior.*

Millman, Dan. (1991) *Sacred Journey of the Peaceful Warrior*.

Millman, Dan. (1992) *No ordinary Moments: A Peaceful Warrior's Guide to Daily Life*.

Millman, Dan. (1995) *The Life You Were Born To Live*.

Millman, Dan. (1999) *Everyday Enlightenment*.

Morgan, Marlo. (1995) *Mutant Message Down Under*.

Morgan, Marlo. (1998) *Mutant Messages From Forever: A Novel of Aboriginal Wisdom*.

Nichols, L. Joseph. (2000) *The Soul As Healer: Lessons in Affirmation, Visualization and Inner Power*.

Peniel, Jon. (1998) *The Lost Teachings of Atlantis: The Children of The Law of One*.

Peniel, Jon. (1999) *The Golden Rule Workbook: A Manual for the New Millennium*.

Price, John Randolph. (1987) *The Superbeings*.

Price, John Randolph. (1998) *The Success Book*.

Quinn, Gary. (2003) *Experience Your Greatness: Give Yourself Permission To Live*. (Audio CD)

Redfield, James. (1995) *The Celestine Prophecy*.

Redfield, James. (1997) *The Celestine Vision: Living the New Spiritual Awareness*.

Redfield, James. (1998) *The Tenth Insight*.

Redfield, James. (1999) *The Secret of Shambhala*.

Renard, Gary. (2004) *The Disappearance of the Universe*.

Renard, Gary. (2006) *Your Immortal Reality: How To Break the Cycle of Birth and Death*.

Ruiz, Don Miguel. (1997) *The Four Agreements: A Practical Guide to Personal Freedom*.

Ruiz, Don Miguel. (1999) *The Mastery of Love: A Practical Guide to The Art of Relationship*.

Ruiz, Don Miguel. (2000) *The Four Agreements Companion Book*.

Ruiz, Don Miguel. (2004) *The Voice of Knowledge: A Practical Guide to Inner Peace*.

Ruiz, Don Miguel. (2009) *Fifth Agreement: A Practical Guide to Self-Mastery.*

Schuman, Helen. (1997) *A Course in Miracles.*

Schwartz, Robert. (2009) *Your Soul's Plan: Discovering the Real Meaning of the Life You Planned Before You Were Born.*

Sharma, Robin. (1997) *The Monk Who Sold His Ferrari.*

Sharma, Robin. (2005) *Big Ideas to Live Your Best Life: Discover Your Destiny.*

Shinn, Florence Scovel. (1989) *The Wisdom of Florence Scovel Shinn.*

Shinn, Florence Scovel. (1991) *The Game of Life Affirmation and Inspiration Cards: Positive Words For A Positive Life.*

Shinn, Florence Scovel. (2006) *The Game of Life.* (Book and CD)

Tolle, Eckhart. (1999) *The Power of Now: A Guide to Spiritual Enlightenment.*

Tolle, Eckhart. (2001) *Practicing the Power of Now: Meditations, Exercises and Core Teachings for Living the Liberated Life.*

Tolle, Eckhart. (200_) *The Realization of Being: A Guide to Experiencing Your True Identity.* (Audio CD)

Tolle, Eckhart. (2002) *Stillness Speaks.*

Tolle, Eckhart. (2003) *Entering The Now.* (Audio CD)

Tolle, Eckhart. (2005) *A New Earth: Awakening to Your Life's Purpose.*

Twyman, James. (1998) *Emissary of Peace: A Vision of Light.*

Twyman, James. (2000) *The Secret of the Beloved Disciple.*

Twyman, James. (2000) *Portrait of the Master.*

Twyman, James. (2000) *Praying Peace: In Conversation with Gregg Braden and Doreen Virtue.*

Twyman, James. (2003) *The Proposing Tree.*

Twyman, James. (2008) *The Moses Code: The Most Powerful Manifestation Tool in the History of the World.*

Twyman, James. (2009) *The Kabbalah Code: A True Adventure.*

Twyman, James. (2009) *The Proof: A 40-Day Program for Embodying Oneness.*

Vanzant, Iyanla. (2000) *Until Today.*

Virtue, Doreen. (1997) *The Lightworker's Way.*

Virtue, Doreen. (2006) *Divine Magic: The Seven Sacred Secrets of Manifestation.* (Book and CD)

Walker, Ethan III. (2003) *The Mystic Christ: The Light of Non-Duality and the Path of Love According to the Life and Teachings of Jesus.*

Walsch, Neale Donald. (1999) *Abundance and Right Livelihood: Applications for Living.*

Walsch, Neale Donald. (2000) *Bringers of The Light.*

Walsch, Neale Donald. (2002) *The New Revelations: A Conversation with God.*

Walters, J. Donald. (2000) *Awaken to Superconsciousness: How To Use Meditation for Inner Peace, Intuitive Guidance and Greater Awareness.*

Walters, J. Donald. (2000) *Meditations to Awaken Superconsciousness: Guided Meditations on The Light* (audio cassette).

Walters, J. Donald. (2003) *Meditation for Starters*. (Book and CD)

Walters, J. Donald. (2003) *Metaphysical Meditations*. (Audio CD)

Walters, J. Donald. (2003) *Secrets of Bringing Peace On Earth*.

Weiss, Brian. (2001) *Messages From the Masters: Tapping Into The Power of Love*.

Weiss, Brian. (2002) *Meditation: Achieving Inner Peace and Tranquility in Your Life*.

Williamson, Marianne. (1996) *A Return To Love*.

Williamson, Marianne. (1997) *Morning and Evening Meditations and Prayers*.

Williamson, Marianne. (2002) *Everyday Grace: Having Hope, Finding Forgiveness and Making Miracles*.

Williamson, Marianne. (2003) *Being In Light*. (Audio CD set)

Yogananda, Paramahansa. (1979) *Metaphysical Meditations: Universal Prayers, Affirmations and Visualizations.*

Yogananda, Paramahansa. (2004) *The Second Coming of Christ: The Resurrection of the Christ Within You.*

Zukav, Gary. (1998) *The Seat of The Soul.*

Zukav, Gary. (2001) *Thoughts from The Seat of The Soul: Meditations for Souls in Process.*

Zukav, Gary and Francis, Linda. (2001) *The Heart of The Soul: Emotional Awareness.*

Zukav, Gary and Francis, Linda. (2003) *The Mind of The Soul: Responsible Choice.*

Zukav, Gary and Francis, Linda. (2003) *Self-Empowerment Journal: A Companion to The Mind of The Soul: Responsible Choice.*

Zukav, Gary. (2010) *Spiritual Partnership: The Journey to Authentic Power.*

Michele Doucette is webmistress of *Portals of Spirit*, a spirituality website whereby one will find links to (1) *The Enlightened Scribe*, (2) an ezine called *Gateway To The Soul*, (3) books of spiritual resonance as well as authors of metaphysical importance, (4) categories of interest from Angels to Zen, (5) up-to-date information as shared by a Quantum Healer, (6) affiliate programs and resources of personal significance, (7) healing resource advertisements and (8) spiritual news.

As a Level 2 Reiki Practitioner, she sends long distance Reiki to those who make the request, claiming only to be a *facilitator of the Universal Energy*, meaning that it is up to the individual(s) in question to use these energies in order to heal themselves.

Having also acquired a Crystal Healing Practitioner diploma (Stonebridge College in the UK), she is guardian to many from the mineral kingdom. In keeping, she has written *The Wisdom of Crystals* which is offered as an ebook on her website.

The author of several other spiritual/metaphysical tomes; namely, *The Ultimate Enlightenment For 2012: All We Need Is Ourselves* and *Turn Off The TV: Turn On Your Mind.*

In addition, she has also written *A Travel in Time to Grand Pré*, a visionary metaphysical title that historically ties the descendants of Yeshua to modern day Nova Scotia.

Against the backdrop of 1754 Acadie, it was the blending of French Acadian history with current DNA testing that allowed for the weaving of this alchemical tale of time travel, romance and intrigue.

From Henry I Sinclair to the Merovingians, from the Cathari treasure at Montségur to the Knights Templar, this novel, together with the words of Yeshua as spoken at the height of his ministry, has the potential to inspire others; for it is herein that we learn how individuals can find their way, their truth(s), so as to live their lives to the fullest.

www.ingramcontent.com/pod-product-compliance
Lightning Source LLC
Chambersburg PA
CBHW061432040426
42450CB00007B/1010